THE

BOOK

OF

MALCOLM

THE

BOOK

OF

MALCOLM

My Son's Life with Schizophrenia

FRASER SUTHERLAND

Foreword by Carmine Starnino

RARE MACHINES

Publisher: Scott Fraser | Acquiring editor: Russell Smith
Cover designer: David Drummond
Printer: Marquis Book Printing Inc.

Library and Archives Canada Cataloguing in Publication

Title: The book of Malcolm : my son's life with schizophrenia / Fraser Sutherland ; foreword by Carmine Starnino.
Names: Sutherland, Fraser, author. | Starnino, Carmine, writer of foreword.
Identifiers: Canadiana (print) 20210297557 | Canadiana (ebook) 20210297913 | ISBN 9781459749566 (softcover) | ISBN 9781459749573 (PDF) | ISBN 9781459749580 (EPUB)
Subjects: LCSH: Sutherland, Malcolm, -2009. | LCSH: Sutherland, Malcolm, -2009—Mental health. | LCSH: Schizophrenics—Canada—Biography. | LCSH: Schizophrenics—Family relationships—Canada—Biography. | LCSH: Sutherland, Fraser—Family. | LCSH: Parent and adult child—Canada. | CSH: Authors, Canadian (English)—Biography. | LCGFT: Biographies.
Classification: LCC RC514 .S88 2022 | DDC 616.89/80092—dc23

We acknowledge the support of the Canada Council for the Arts and the Ontario Arts Council for our publishing program. We also acknowledge the financial support of the Government of Ontario, through the Ontario Book Publishing Tax Credit and Ontario Creates, and the Government of Canada.

Printed and bound in Canada.

Rare Machines, an imprint of Dundurn Press
1382 Queen Street East
Toronto, Ontario, Canada M4L 1C9
dundurn.com, @dundurnpress

FOREWORD

Carmine Starnino

A s a wolfish young critic, hungry to offend, I loved Fraser Sutherland's thought crimes. Margaret Atwood's famous critical study *Survival* was "the most misleading thematic summary ever perpetrated against a gullible public." Anne Carson, for all her international laurels, was a poet of "distracting academic archness and clutter." Jack Hodgins's celebrated fiction was "tiresomely ramified melodrama." Sheila Watson's classic novel *Double Hook* "surely rivals Leonard Cohen's *Beautiful Losers* for unreadability" (a lovely, and rare, trick of the double takedown).

Fraser was, no denying it, a tough customer. He reviewed books mostly for the *Globe and Mail*, and in interviews he seemed toughest on colleagues willing to give everything a free pass — a club I was determined not to join. ("I'm dismayed," he once said, "at how little independence and real dissent gets expressed.") But what also caught my eye when reading him were the parts of his writing that caught my ear. The man could turn a phrase. What went into that phrase-turning was a lifetime revelling in language. Fraser earned his living as a freelancer, where fluency is currency. Starting out as a reporter and staff writer in 1970s, he transformed himself into a formidable literary journalist. A self-taught lexicographer, he edited and wrote definitions for dictionaries. Sometime in the 2000s, he set up a side hustle as a brand-name consultant, coining names for companies and products. Fraser's appreciation of words as "physical items" with "weight and volume, drag and propulsion" led to a style that joined precision and plain sense — a style that, as I learned when we became friends, extended to his personality.

Fraser was rarely over-awed; rather, he was tetchy. He was also funny in a way that wasn't always funny, but wary. He had a wit that kept everything down to earth. He was a useful corrective, always subtly right-sizing the few enthusiasms I allowed myself. "You are especially generous to the young and starting-out," he warned me in an email, "who of course should be discouraged as much as possible." He had lived all over the country — Halifax, Ottawa, Montreal, and Nelson, B.C., before settling in Toronto with his wife and son — and picked up an alarming store of literary gossip, the most damning from the late 1960s and '70s. Watching him, over a pint, drop a tell-all anecdote about a Famous Canadian Writer wasn't just entertaining: it helped strip away any illusion about reputations. It's hard to believe in the showbiz version of CanLit when you know a bit about the quasi-incestuous pile-on of its early days.

There was something wonderfully ad hoc and unsystematic about Fraser's mind. He once described himself as a "displaced, unreconstructed Nova Scotian farm boy," and the breadth of subjects he followed (and reviewed, with authority) showed that he put no restraints on his enthusiasms. Sutherland was also obsessive. A natural researcher, the fear of excluding a detail often overtook him. His book-length poem, *Jonestown*, took fifteen years to complete; his biography of poet Edward Lacey, twelve.

Fraser's insights felt hard-won. They also, I wager, came at a cost. There was a sadness to him — the sadness of a man who tried hard to tell the truth; the kind of truth that was always unfashionable. Fraser often seemed alone, even among friends (and sometimes especially). That sadness got into his poems, which explored ideas of exile and self-isolation, and which seemed written (at least to me) in his darker hours. "Connecting with the other," he once said, "is a way of connecting with the otherness within myself." Fraser's activities as a literary arbiter and self-declared "counterpuncher" so coloured his career that it could be surprising to see what his poems were up to. The close-at-hand observations ("I awoke this morning to a solitary chainsaw / cracking and ripping the country air"), the head-clearing insights ("These are days when I would want to begin again / in some stranger-city"), the raw moments remembered and reflected on ("First I was lonely / Then I was depressed.") While he sometimes tried out more bardic tones, his voice had little of the ego-posturing he loathed in contemporary poetry. In fact, the curmudgeon could be downright disarming:

> *When we talk, you'll notice*
> *I do not look directly*
> *at you but downward or ahead, my good ear*
> *inclined toward your words, now*
> *and then glancing briefly at you to affirm*
> *I am still listening, still there.*

Those lines, which open "Looking Away," show no trace of the self-important demands of a busy career as an editor and critic.

They are not the lines of someone who wants to win over juries or who is fighting to stay in the swim of a literary scene ("If the trappings of public success, however welcome, began to descend on me," he said in an interview, "I'd start to suspect myself"). They belong to a man who wants to say a few meaningful words about being in the world. The best of Fraser's poems are quiet dramas of distress. You wouldn't call them candid; they are vulnerable, unsentimental, confiding — "as if unwittingly / he's strayed into a life." They take on modest, uninflated forms, finding "the truth a foot in front of me."

Many of us assumed that truth-finding ended when Fraser died on March 28, 2021, at the age of seventy-four. But Fraser, having outlived his wife by three years, had completed a memoir about their only son, who was diagnosed with schizophrenia in his late teens and then died suddenly at twenty-six. Part elegy, part existential howl, *The Book of Malcolm* is an investigation of a beloved child's life, of the moods and registers of his mental illness, and of their sometimes harrowing moments as a family. It is also a coda to a body of work defined by the refusal to compromise. In his grief, Fraser has forged sentences of unbearable lucidity. This prose — bracing, probing, pin-sharp — is his final gift to us. In a poem called "Abdals," he pondered the mysterious figures of Sufi lore "through whom the world is able to continue its existence." Abdals are "secret sharers of provided-for benevolence" whose good works hold up the universe. When one dies, God appoints another. *The Book of Malcolm* is the book of an Abdal, but I can't see how he will ever be replaced.

*

Carmine Starnino's most recent book of poetry is Dirty Words: Selected Poems 1997–2016. *He lives in Montreal.*

PART ONE

ON THE EVENING of Christmas Day 2009, I wished my son Malcolm good night as he lay on the cracked leather couch in the living room, apparently watching that Christmas perennial, Frank Capra's *It's a Wonderful Life*, on TV. It had been years since I'd seen it, so I wasn't even sure he was watching the eventful story of George Bailey, family man and small-town banker, played by James Stewart. In the wake of his bank's calamitous failure Bailey is crushed by despair. But a good angel makes him understand how important he'd been to everyone.

Malcolm looked weary, slightly disturbed, with a slightly puzzled frown. I wondered what was going through his mind. Wondering what was going through Malcolm's mind had become my preoccupation in recent years. Did he think he had his own good angel hovering at that moment?

∗

THE EARLY MORNING of Boxing Day, my wife, Alison, schooled by her mother, Althea, to give false cheer at all times, said, "This is the best Christmas ever. I'd give it eight out of ten." I grumbled, "Well, the wonder is it happened at all."

The weeks leading up to it had been filled with minor misfortunes. Not long after we bought a sleek, cappuccino-coloured Burmese cat and named him Lancaster — after a Hollywood star or a British heavy bomber — it had become apparent he had the looks of Mel Gibson but the brains of a gopher. Someone said it could have been worse: he could have had the brains of Mel Gibson. Brainless Lancaster had bolted out the open back door as, oblivious, Alison left for work in the early morning dark. He hadn't been seen since. Malcolm phoned his former girlfriend Marie to light a candle for Lancaster at her Roman Catholic cathedral.

At my urging we searched everywhere: behind curtains and bookshelves, under couches and beds, in the depths of blankets, among pots and pans on the kitchen shelves. And in the basement, behind the furnace and the freezer, in between boxes and file cartons. I probed into deep boxes heaped with clothing and even poked at the plastic sheet insulation stapled across the ceiling. Crazily, I even looked in the freezer. It bothered me that Malcolm was not looking hard enough. His search seemed perfunctory, as if he already knew my quest was hopeless and had resigned himself to loss. We taped the breeder's photo of Lancaster with our phone number on hydro poles up and down the street. No call came. It seemed impossible he could survive the subzero Toronto nights.

Hoping that Lancaster would luck into a warm house, Malcolm wondered if we had done something wrong, incurring bad karma, worried that he in particular had brought it about. Karma — desires, intentions, attitudes, deeds good and bad — all had material, moral, and spiritual effects. Even before Lancaster vanished we'd lost another cat, struck by a car. When Malcolm meditated, as he often did, it felt weird, he wrote in his diary, because he felt so sad.

That Christmas Eve we were late in putting up a tree lugged from the corner convenience store. Alison couldn't find the box of ornaments from my boyhood home in rural Nova Scotia, including the tiny, wire-becapped Santa Claus that topped the tree. I'd inherited it. Then she remembered that in a fit of basement clearing she and her obliging but mentally handicapped brother had thrown it out. To make do she stuck decorative odds and ends on the branches. Malcolm remarked it was strange that people celebrate Christmas around a tree that in fact is slowly dying.

Little and not so little things going wrong. A kitchen cupboard door falls off its hinges. Alison loses her wallet with her driver's licence, health card, and credit cards.

I went with her to hire a car, pretending I'd be the driver. I was inept at city driving, but of course the car-rental place didn't know that. Now the car sat in the lane parking spot behind our backyard next to a big eastward-leaning Manitoba maple. The next day Alison was going to drive us an hour and a half to the city of Peterborough. From time immemorial her parents, siblings, aunts, uncles, and cousins had gathered on Boxing Day to gorge on turkey and gravy and all the other fixings of a festive dinner people brought: the yellow and green vegetables, the cranberry sauce, the hard sauce for the plum pudding, the mince pie. It was an eccentric custom. About everybody middle-class of our skin colour would have had had their big Christmas dinner the day before. Not Alison's family. After we gorged, we played giddy party games.

*

FOREMOST AMONG MISHAPS large and small prior to Boxing Day was Malcolm's seizure. Late one morning I was in my office upstairs; Alison was away at work. Malcolm was in the bathroom next door, drying his hair after a bath before setting off for his noon-to-five job at a print shop. I heard a crash. Outside my door I found him on his side on the floor, half against the wall, half against a bookcase. His arms and legs, hands and feet, were convulsing. When I spoke to him he did not respond. I phoned 9-1-1 and answered questions, dashing back and forth to the hall to check on him. His arms and legs were still shaking. He still did not respond. When I next returned to the hall he was no longer there.

After a few moments of panic looking for him I found him in his own room in his own bed. He had stopped convulsing. At first he could not answer me, and then only brokenly. Mostly he groaned: his back was hurting badly. He kept trying to sit up, falling back in agony. I paced, waiting for the paramedics. They were taking their time; twenty minutes passed. At last they arrived. By now Malcolm was lucid.

Strapped to a stretcher, he went by ambulance to St. Michael's Hospital Emergency. I phoned Alison at work. She said she'd see us at St. Michael's. In the Emergency Ward I found him strapped to a bed. He complained the restraints wouldn't allow him to breathe. Nobody paid any attention to him. Alison arrived and they took him away for an X-ray and an MRI. I didn't have time to cancel an appointment with someone I was supposed to meet that day. After I briefly saw him and rushed back to the ward, Alison and Malcolm had just left. I spotted them in the back of a taxi in time to catch them, Malcolm stuffed and stiffened with painkillers.

The next day I phoned his psychiatrist at her clinic in the west-end Parkdale neighbourhood where we used to live and where Malcolm had spent his first two years. It was a misery getting him there in a cab to her distant office. We had to stop often so he could

THE BOOK OF MALCOLM

try to retch. When we got there he drooled and slurred his words. The last thing he recalled from before the seizure was drying his hair. Dr. D. wrote out prescriptions, maintaining the antipsychotic medication he'd been phasing out of since September, reducing the new medication he'd been phasing into.

Over the next few days it was a struggle to get him to move around, as I'd been told he should. Still in pain, he showed up at his job in the print shop. We saw the psychiatrist again, and she spent time with him alone. We took a streetcar and bought Christmas Eve and Christmas Day food in Kensington Market and in a Chinese supermarket. While waiting to buy oysters, we watched the man behind the fish counter scoop out a large fish from a tank. He hurled it to the cement floor and, while it madly flopped, clubbed it to death. Malcolm, a gentle vegetarian, stood there appalled. It could have been worse. Once in a Chinese supermarket I'd seen someone take a cleaver and bisect a frog on a butcher's block.

We hurried off for an appointment with a St. Michael's neurologist, a follow-up to our ER visit. The neurologist gave him a brief physical exam ("How many fingers?"). He said it wouldn't be rewarding to seek complicated reasons for the seizure since it was a known side effect of the antipsychotic he'd been placed on and which in fact had been working well. The answer was to reduce the dosage. This had been done already. I got our family doctor to deal with the ongoing back pain. He prescribed something.

We went home. It had been a three-doctor day.

*

CHRISTMAS EVE, A dusting of snow. The three of us walked to a carol service in a beige stucco building on the corner, the Christian Church, Disciples of Christ. That was the denomination the sinister Rev. Jim Jones had contaminated, turning a branch of it into his

Peoples Temple. This mild-mannered Toronto branch was unlikely to be a site for a mass suicide.

We didn't belong to the church but it was convenient — and inoffensive enough — to attend. I got the time wrong and we arrived too early. We retreated home for half an hour. When we returned, poinsettias adorning the sanctuary had been placed "in memory of loved ones." Pretty Filipinas, slimmer versions of Malcolm's former girlfriend, read scripture, and we sang carols, led by a lanky clownlike elder cheerfully urging us on in "Come All Ye Faithful" and "Joy to the World." At the end there was to be communion, but Alison and I left. Malcolm elected to stay on. Afterward, I asked him whether he'd taken communion. He said he hadn't. Why not? He said he didn't know.

Since for decades Alison's family had had their big dinner on Boxing Day, Christmas Day would not be turkey-with-all-the-trimmings. On Christmas morning came our own ritual of unwrapping boxes, thriftily stuffing the paper into a garbage bag for use on the presents we were going to give next year. Alison's brother turned up to get presents from his four sisters, and Alison got presents, too. Darcy, our standard poodle ("substandard poodle," we liked to say), stood around tensely, eager to get his teeth on the wrapping paper. A joke present to me from Alison: Donald Trump and Bill Zanker, *Think Big: Make It Happen in Business and Life.* As expected, a box of Turtles for me. I was fond of the caramel-wrapped pecans, but I disliked giving and receiving gifts. One seldom knew what to buy for anybody and always had to pretend to be delighted at what one got, no matter what. Alison always said I hated buying presents but was good at it. Malcolm said, "Oh, Dad loves to do the things he hates." I'd got him a little Irish sterling-silver cross because he'd always liked Celtic mythology, and an electric beard-trimmer, because it was on his want-list. His beard was just long enough to be trimmed.

Malcolm was always fastidious, keen on looking good; like his paternal Uncle Bill that way.

He gave me a cigar, a cigar-cutter, and a couple of packets of pipe tobacco. With mock severity, he warned me to use the tobacco sparingly. At school the kids had been hectored against smoking; he'd always railed against my smoking, and I'd had to refrain from puffing on my pipe in any room he was in. So this present must have been a last resort, just as the Christmas gift to my own father, pipe tobacco, always was a last resort because he'd never say what he wanted. Maybe he didn't want to admit he wanted anything. Maybe I didn't either.

Later that day, Malcolm tried out the beard-trimmer, converting his short, reddish beard into a tidy Van Dyke. Like Alison's brother and my brother, he had red hair. He asked me how he looked. I didn't normally approve of Van Dykes but on him it looked good. My brother phoned him from North Carolina, where he was spending the holidays with his girlfriend.

I'd invited a few people to come over that afternoon. One was Natasha, a petite, dark, Bosnian girl who'd shared an apartment with my friend Goran, who was just now in Croatia. When she first came round Malcolm had taken a shine to her, and she to him. They'd been having long talks and taking long walks together.

I wasn't sure she'd show up because her plans were always in flux and the old car Goran had left with her had broken down. I could never think of Goran without bringing to mind Frank Sinatra's "Call Me Irresponsible," but there was a selfless side to him, too. The previous summer he had given Malcolm driving lessons. They would creep up and down the lane behind the house, round the block, circle inside a vacant school parking lot. Goran reported Malcolm had been nervous, which of course made Goran nervous, too. Sometimes Natasha would take him for a drive while Goran and I drank Scotch in my kitchen. Since Alison no longer owned a car, we thought of buying Goran's, except his unpaid parking tickets had piled up.

When Natasha left at the end of the afternoon on Christmas Day it was pouring rain. Malcolm wanted to walk her home, but she assured him it wasn't necessary and he should rest his back. He must have asked at least three times, telling her he didn't feel like a gentleman letting her walk alone.

Stragglers left. Malcolm settled down on the couch to watch the movie. He was watching it when Alison went to bed early, as was her custom, and was still watching it when I did.

A few days earlier, he and I had been walking up our street. He'd said, "When you saw me having the seizure, it must have been terrifying." I said, "Yes, it was. I thought you were dying on me." He said, "You won't get rid of me that easy."

A joke, like any one of the thousands we'd shared. I chuckled. A few days later he was dead.

IN THE MORNING I assembled twenty pounds of silken mashed potatoes, molecules of hot milk fused with molecules of white potatoes, making a kind of solidified vichyssoise. It was my usual contribution to the Boxing Day party.

I was in my office upstairs when Alison went to wake Malcolm up so we could be on our way to Peterborough. A moment later I heard a scream of the kind I had never heard from Alison or from anyone else. It was a sound I never wanted to hear again. She rushed in and cried, "Malcolm's dead!" I mumbled "I don't believe it" and ran to his room. He lay turned on his side in bed, his mouth half open, his eyes closed. When I touched his shoulder, it was hard, solid, cold. There was no doubt in my mind he was dead. The

9-1-1 operator asked calmly, "Is he breathing?" "No," I said. The voice told me to put him on his back; I was to give him CPR. He was heavy — weight gain was one side effect of an antipsychotic he'd been taking. Tumbling his naked body slowly from the bed to the floor was easily done. Alison gasped. On his torso were huge, discoloured blotches.

This time the paramedics came almost at once. Past the barking poodle, they tramped upstairs. It didn't take them long to say what we already knew. Two policemen arrived, joined by a police detective and a coroner. The detective asked us questions and put all pills in a plastic bag. The blotches had come from the pooling of blood, he explained, and meant Malcolm had died some hours earlier.

Alison asked to stay with his body for a while. In cases like this one — not that there was a precedent — I often thought she was acting a role, playing a part in which she'd cast herself. As if up to and including now she had acted and directed in the dress rehearsal for death called life. I was being unfair. In these circumstances who said I had to be fair? I had no desire to linger, just as I had refused to go to a funeral home, pompous phrase, for the visitation, pompous word, after my mother died. I couldn't connect the living Malcolm with the dead weight lying on the floor.

Liza, one of Alison's sisters, arrived. She said the paramedics, or whatever they were, asked us not to watch while they took Malcolm's body away. "In the body bag," I said. "They're afraid of hysterics?" As a writer it seemed more important to me to register this event than to embarrass or inconvenience anybody. Liza opened a closet door, partly blocking the view. I closed it.

We sat in the kitchen while the paramedics slowly bumped down the stairs. Then they were gone. One policeman remained, sitting silent in our bedroom until he could ask us questions in privacy.

*

IT HAD ONLY taken a phone call or two and our small living room began to fill. People huddled on the sofa, drifted in and out, arrived and left. Bad news did indeed travel fast. Polly, another out-of-town sister who would not be going to the Boxing Day party, appeared. She said she'd contact the funeral home that had handled several family funerals. "Whoa, whoa, whoa!" I shouted. I did not want to get locked into commitments. "Displacement activity," she admitted. Natasha turned up, weeping. Her tears took over the room; women hugged her. A phone call came from Goran in Zagreb. I phoned Malcolm's godfather Adrian in Montreal, an antiquarian bookseller. "That's *terrible!*" he said, breaking down.

At some point I told people there was Malcolm, and there were Malcolm's problems. And that, though the problems were gone, somehow one still wanted them. They'd mean he was alive. Where there were problems it meant they could be resolved. When they asked me if I wanted company, I said it was hard to talk to people. It was harder still to be alone.

*

ON MONDAY, EVA, our Polish cleaning lady, arrived before eight as usual. She and Malcolm had long maintained a raucous, jokey relationship. He once asked her to say something very rude in Polish. Thereafter he'd sing it out, often while in the shower, in a powerful operatic bass. With much uproar, she in piercing shouts, he replying in overdone groans, she would turf him out of bed so she could clean his room. Now I asked her to sit down. "What's wrong?" she asked. I told her, and she began to weep.

*

A FEW OF the friends with whom I drank beer on Tuesday nights at the Beverley Tavern came, kindly urging me to join them that week. Surely they knew I wouldn't. I supposed it was something for them to say. They stood around the kitchen, glasses in hand, trying to maintain the cheerful mood of so many uneventful tavern evenings. It was hopeless.

That night, the house seething with people, I heard from down the hall Alison's carrying shout. "Lancaster's back!" A neighbour from up the street held the missing Burmese in his arms. He and his wife had the custom of feeding strays, and they'd noticed an odd-looking cat among them. They connected him with the picture on our missing-cat poster. Hoarsely purring, Lancaster had lost almost half his weight, but was otherwise healthy. How he managed to survive two weeks of freezing nights, he who had never been outside in his lifetime other than to win cat shows and commute to a summer cottage, we couldn't imagine. Malcolm, as pet-obsessed as his parents, would have rejoiced. But perhaps he would have taken it as a normal miracle.

Without consciously trying, Alison and I played the roles of the bereaved, no matter how strained and strange it seemed. Implicitly, without talking about it, we separately resolved we would accept what people had to offer, that we would not refuse anyone's friendship, that we would not take offence at whatever anyone said, no matter how clumsy, clichéd, or outrightly stupid. They would usually start, "I don't know what to say ..." One had to recognize this was true, and go on from there. Alison said it was our responsibility to comfort them as much as it was to be comforted. In fact, the best comfort to me, inasmuch as there could be any, was to do something for someone else, even if it was only to thank them for a gift. And the gifts began to arrive — food, drink, flowers. Our fridge overflowed with quiches and cheeses. The big pot of cold mashed potatoes on the unlit burner at the back of the stove began to ferment. After a couple of days a friend tasted it and said it was going sour. I took a forkful. She was right. I dumped it in the composter.

It seemed such a waste.

*

WE WEREN'T JEWISH, but for a week we sat shiva from morning till night. It wasn't like the Nova Scotia afternoons following a funeral, survivors sitting in a vacuumed living room in their best, receiving the neighbours. It was much more active than that. I was internalizing everything, but Alison was externalizing. She was laughing, whooping, telling stories. All this displacement and denial activity, all this ambient noise, went on around me. Though it was so alien it did not bother me or seem inappropriate. It seemed necessary for her, perhaps for others, too.

The consequence was not just physical but mental exhaustion. For a couple of days I couldn't eat much, and I kept my social exchanges brief, fueled by Scotch. Never quite drunk, I was able to talk more freely than I usually did. At ten or eleven o'clock, dulled by the drink people had brought, I went to bed. I slept soundly. I had never supposed we knew so many people, that we had sunk roots so deeply in the neighbourhood in the seventeen years we had lived there. Phone calls came from people I had not spoken to in months, years, decades. Alison made a point of contacting all the doctors who had treated Malcolm in five and a half years, and we got calls from our pharmacist, recent psychiatrists, and from the neurologist who had seen him days before he died.

The unworthy thought that the professionals were covering themselves against a malpractice suit flickered across my mind. But when one or two people asked who we were going to sue, we brusquely dismissed the idea. Everything in Malcolm's last weeks had followed routine and fulfilled, at least partly, people's good intentions. Even if I had watched for it, no one seemed to have done anything obviously wrong. Nothing could contradict the fact of death. To look for causes, which our friends naturally did, seemed an irrelevance. The coroner who did the autopsy said there'd been no obvious trauma. Malcolm apparently had a seizure. What had caused it? An answer, or perhaps no answer at all, would come from the toxicology report, the blood work, and we might not see it for months.

What was it like to have a seizure? Could anyone say except the person who'd had one, and how could they do that? It was like the celebrated philosophy question, "What is it like to be a bat?" Malcolm hadn't remembered what the first seizure was like. I hoped against hope the second one had been sudden and painless, outside conscious awareness. What could pain mean in such circumstances, when you were no longer aware you were you? It was a question that once might have interested Malcolm intellectually.

*

BETWEEN CHRISTMAS AND New Year's there was a lot to do. I put a death notice in the *Globe and Mail* for the record, to come out the day before the funeral, which we decided would be on Saturday, the day after New Year's Day. It read, in part:

Sutherland, Malcolm Patrick
1984–2009
After a happy Christmas Day, Malcolm Sutherland died in his sleep in Toronto, about two weeks short of his twenty-sixth birthday. He was a graduate in reli-gion and philosophy from Trinity College, University of Toronto, and a volunteer with the ALS Society

of Ontario. For more than five years he had bravely struggled with psychosis, and was making a remarkable recovery. Considerate employers and good friends helped him. No one could have been a gentler person. He was witty, observant, sensitive and deeply spiritual …

*

WE WENT TO see Father Jeff, the bluff, cheerful priest at St. Michael and All Angels, the Anglican church of mostly Caribbean parishioners that we had attended when we moved to Toronto from Nova Scotia. Alison had once been in the choir and been part-time church secretary. After she got a job in the headquarters of the United Church and began attending chapel there, we had fallen away. Sitting in the priest's office, we picked hymns and scripture passages.

"A Thanksgiving for the Life of Malcolm Patrick Sutherland 1984-2009" the program began, adhering to the template. We were no longer supposed to grieve; we were supposed to give thanks. We picked "Be Thou My Vision," with its lovely Irish tune, Alison's favourite hymn. The scripture passage that spoke most forcibly to me was Romans 8:22–26:

> For we know that the whole creation groaneth and travaileth in pain together until now.
>
> And not only they, but ourselves also, which have the firstfruits of the Spirit, even we ourselves groan within ourselves, waiting for the adoption, to wit, the redemption of our body.
>
> For we are saved by hope: but hope that is seen is not hope; for what a man seeth, why doth he yet hope for?

But if we hope for that we see not, then do we with patience wait for it.

Likewise the Spirit also helpeth our infirmities: for we know not what we should pray for as we ought: but the Spirit itself maketh intercession for us with groanings which cannot be uttered.

The hymn "Lead Kindly Light." The Sermon on the Mount with the Beatitudes: "Blessed are the poor in spirit: for theirs is the kingdom of heaven." Matthew 5:1–12. And, ending the service, "Immortal, Invisible, God Only Wise" ("*Unresting, unhasting, and silent as light*"). One Christmas season the multitalented Jonathan Miller had heard a Salvation Army brass band play that hymn in the distance and put it into his TV play *Alice in Wonderland*. Hearing it now brought one of many improbable aspects of Malcolm back to me, as did the sound of Ravi Shankar playing an involuted melody on the sitar.

We set aside time and space for Malcolm's friends to talk about him without being rushed. Already several had said they wanted to, and on Facebook Malcolm from beyond the grave invited all to "The Grand Farewell" on Saturday, January 2, at 1:00 p.m. I didn't know who had posted the invitation, but it had the self-mocking, satirically self-inflationary note he'd always cultivated.

*

ALISON SEARCHED THE World Wide Web for a cremation firm; a simpler, less expensive alternative to a funeral parlour and all its paraphernalia. She found one at half the usual cost. A man came one evening and we signed papers.

Throughout the week I was on the phone to my brother Bill, vacationing in North Carolina with his girlfriend. People were asking if he was going to attend the funeral. He dithered about whether to attend. He thought he might return to hometown Halifax and fly up a week later, which he said would give him time to be alone with us, undistracted by the emotional claims of people at the funeral. It seemed to me a form of moral cowardice but I didn't insist he come. It would have been counterproductive anyway. A younger brother does not change an older brother's mind.

*

EVERY DAY THAT week was difficult; each had the potential to be the hardest yet. Perhaps Tuesday morning, on the second day of visitors, was the worst. Malcolm's psychiatrist and a psychiatric nurse came. The psychiatrist, whom Malcolm had liked more than any of the many he'd had, was unaffectedly sweet. She'd been fond of him, as she wasn't with many patients experiencing psychosis she had to deal with. We would sit in the clinic waiting room, waiting for her to call us out from among the mumblers, the dazed self-absorbed listening to mantras only they could hear. Back in September she had suggested Malcolm start a medication, Clozaril, a long-tried antipsychotic that was new to him, phasing out risperidone, on which he'd reached a plateau of no progress. Malcolm's obvious intelligence showed his potential, she said. She thought we should be more aggressive. Now, distressed, she spoke of their agreeable time together.

Malcolm's employer, who ran a print shop in the ritzy shopping district of Yorkdale, arrived with his quiet, sympathetic wife, who worked with him. He wasn't someone with whom I'd ordinarily feel much in common. But there was something a little out of the ordinary about him: the fact his wife, with whom he had a young son, was Japanese; the fact he hired people with psychiatric problems. I didn't know if he got any financial help from the government for doing it, or whether his predecessor, William Ashley, the upscale china shop that had temporarily employed Malcolm, had got it. At the time the thought crossed my mind — and I wondered whether it had crossed William Ashley's — whether a psychotic might be liable to lay waste to a fortune in fine china. But as a "runner" — bringing items from storage — he'd done well.

Malcolm's print shop boss told him he was the public face of the firm when he made deliveries. Malcolm had been good at remembering names and addresses. I was so used to his absentmindedness and forgetfulness even before he'd had his first psychotic episode that this surprised me. He had done so well his boss even thought he could play an increasing part in the business. I'd once snobbishly thought it ridiculous that prospering at such a job represented progress and promise. Now the prospect Malcolm could become even a low-level employee gladdened me.

*

BILL DECIDED TO come here directly. I was relieved. Therese, our kindly, elderly next-door neighbour, offered to put him up. The evening before the funeral he arrived at the front door, suitcase in hand, trembling. Perhaps, I wondered, it was a sign he felt guilty about not having come to see us for years.

Bill deposited his suitcase next door. Sitting around the kitchen table, we persuaded him to eat something. Malcolm's godfather arrived by train from Montreal, sharing the trip with another old friend, this one coming from Ottawa. A second godfather arrived with a mate in tow. Long ago Ken had been a boyfriend of Alison. His first marriage had been to a woman, the second to the man who was with him. People drifted in and out of the kitchen.

*

THE MORNING OF the funeral I was jittery, though there was little to be nervous about. All I had to do was to put in an appearance. I cleaned out coats from the downstairs hall closet, put in more clothes hangers. I panicked because in our crowded bedroom closet I could not find my good suit. Finally I found a dark blue suit that fit me. It was Malcolm's.

*

SATURDAY, JANUARY 2, was piercingly cold. The church was nearly empty; there were only a couple of faithfully church-going Jamaican women sitting in the pews. Alison and I sat in the front pew; the space in front of us was extra-wide to allow for wheelchair users. Bill, who hadn't a suit with him, sat in shirtsleeves beside us, Malcolm's godfathers in the row behind.

Malcolm's former girlfriend Marie joined us, too: she was asserting her emotional rights. Tall, dark, plump, piously Roman Catholic, she had two Spanish grandparents. Musical, she played the harp, that difficult instrument. She and Malcolm had met through the Centre for Addiction and Mental Health — "CAMH," for short — but her problem was different. She was riding a bipolar pendulum, the condition that used to be called manic depression.

I could hear people behind us quietly assembling. We had told the priest he could expect a spectrum all the way from resolute atheists to devout Christians, Jews, and Muslims, and those who had never thought about religious belief, especially their own. The hired church organist began a solemn refrain. During "Lead, Kindly Light" I shed my first tear since Malcolm's death. The word "angel" had got to me. In my mind I blended it with "gentle," though Alison said she had never thought of him as being especially gentle. Yet it was the word people most often used about him during the week. Malcolm had always been interested in angelology, had so often sought a good angel.

And with the morn those angel faces smile,
Which I have loved long since, and lost awhile!

It was a traditional Anglican service in some ways. A surprisingly large number of people filed forward to take communion. There was no homily. Alison hated homilies. We wanted Malcolm's friends and cousins to speak about him just before the benediction, and to take all the time they wanted. Introducing them, Alison said that the past week, with all the love and friendship that had poured in, had been "the most amazing week of my life." What I found amazing was her courage, poise, and self-control.

Marie was the first of Malcolm's friends to speak. Tearful now and then, she read from a letter he had written her about a year earlier when they broke up. A little dazed, and with my bad hearing, I could not take in much of it except the tender, regretful tone. I did hear her say, "Malcolm was strong, someone who endured so much, yet never once complained. He fought for a long time; that time was never easy. I, and many others were some of the people who were always there for him as he fought, yet we could never really see what deep sorrow lay beneath that frail, yet courageous spirit.... He would always ask me, 'Do you think God is mad at me?' Now that I look back on it, I remember those times, and how pure and innocent he was, humble, yet forgiving."

She said, "Deep down inside, it was hard for Malcolm to hear God's words. His suffering was far too much for anyone to see. Battling schizophrenia wasn't easy, and yet it seemed it was Malcolm's time to be taken back home, to a safe, pure place for him to rest his mind for eternity. Right now as his loved ones are near, Jesus is welcoming him into his new home with God."

It must be quite a crowd, I thought.

We didn't know how many would come up to speak. In the event, there were no awkward pauses. Ashley, his high school girlfriend ("That girl took my virginity," he once told me half satirically, half-nostalgically), read a Shakespeare sonnet. Even through tears, the people his age spoke in clear, projecting voices, and it made me think what fine people they were, so unlike the fuddy-duddy idea I'd had of them as a feckless, directionless generation. Someone from CAMH said kind words about him, though I cynically wondered if it was also a form of public relations. Two of our neighbours spoke. One of them, Roscoe, who used Malcolm as a babysitter, had a lovely silky smooth voice: she'd once done Oil of Olay commercials. Her husband, Kevin, was also an actor. She told how she and Kevin were proudly showing her new baby off when Alison and Malcolm, then about nine, came. Malcolm very gently put his hand over the baby's face, then hurled himself to the ground, screaming. Alison, appalled, apologized. Later the couple indignantly discussed his behaviour. Then they realized he had enacted the "Vulcan Mind Meld" from TV's *Star Trek*, enabling a merge of minds by means of fingertips. They were still in the throes of indignation when the husband thoughtfully remarked, "But you know, the kid's got great timing."

Laughter filled the church.

After the benediction Alison and I paused, uncertain what to do next. Before the service started we had decided we were not going to stand at the door like official greeters. But now Alison thought that we could slip out the side door. I said I'd hung up my coat at the back. Finally, Malcolm's Montreal godfather had the presence of mind to tell us that we should exit by the centre aisle. We did. To my surprise the church was full: there might have been three hundred people in it. As we went, people edged out from the pews and embraced us. It was like being a politician making an entrance to a rally, only in reverse. At the back door, more people hugged me as they departed.

Suddenly Father Jeff cornered me, demanding $125 to pay the impecunious hired organist. I would gladly have paid in advance if

I'd been asked but now I felt like a debtor in a drug deal. I scrabbled in my wallet, emptying it. A hundred dollars: the priest said that would do. Alison and I lingered, people still wanting to talk and hug. With the gay partner of Malcolm's godfather we walked back to our house in the bitter cold.

When we arrived at 39 Helena Avenue, several blocks away, we could hardly get in the door. Malcolm's aunts, uncles, and cousins filled the dining room; a cousin and Alison's sister Polly took charge of the catering. The house was dangerously congested. There was scant room to turn around, even to hang up coats. How anyone could get something to eat or drink I didn't know. I retreated upstairs, as some others had done. "Higher ground," a friend quipped, quoting the spiritual:

> *I'm pressing on the upward way,*
> *New heights I'm gaining every day;*
> *Still praying as I onward bound,*
> *"Lord, plant my feet on higher ground."*

Letters, cards, envelopes with cash, written reminiscences, piled up in the in-tray of my upstairs office. In the evening, more people came, like an Albanian couple who had been away all week and only that day had heard about Malcolm. We sat quietly conversing in the living room; the rest of the house suddenly seemed eerily empty.

The next week a man and woman from the crematorium arrived with a dark-wrapped box, a certificate taped on top. The woman said it had been assigned a number, not a name, to avoid any possible mix-up. The box seemed to weigh ounces, not pounds. For now I put it in a drawer of a file cabinet.

*

NATASHA HAD SAID she wanted to join in the eulogies at Malcolm's memorial service. In the end she lost her nerve. She did, however, email what was in her mind.

> Malcolm was such a sweetheart and he really really understood me and I felt comfortable talking to him (not really easy for me to do) about anything and everything. He just listened with so much compassion and so much love it was just impossible not to feel at ease and completely comfortable and accepted, regardless of what I said ... I thought that he was someone I would like to know for the rest of my life.

Later she wrote:

> Now that I feel alone I know what Malcolm would have told me if he were here to comfort me as he always was. He would again tell me as he once told me before that "the world teaches you that which you are ready to learn and that every lesson comes at exactly the right time." He would also tell me to know that once we have connected with someone's soul that connection never goes away, regardless in what physical space or dimension one is in. I know he would tell me that he is somewhere in a place that is more suited for him at this given time and that this is where he is meant to be right now.

No doubt Natasha was sincere, but in my present mood it sounded like mystical sludge. It didn't register, nor did all the condolence cards, phone calls, emails, and one envoi after another on Facebook. If Malcolm was in another dimension, maybe Facebook could have been it. On it an unknown friend posted: "hey Malcolm.

I'm so sorry I couldn't be at your service today, I just moved to Paris yesterday. I did want to share a photo with you." He and another friend "setup a little shrine in your honour at a techno-party we had last week. We displayed a ton of your photos as well as some bits and pieces of info … bon voyage, mon ami."

We heard from Marie's mother, brother, and sister. From Daniel, the twenty-three-year-old son of Alison's cousin Sheila. From our neighbour Gerald, an artist and art teacher:

> Malcolm and I had a habit of launching into discus-
> sions about the nature of spiritual, the origin of the cos-
> mos and the existence of God as well as various schools
> of philosophical and religious thinking in relation to
> art making and creativity … All this in the middle of
> Helena Avenue as we bumped into each other … both
> of us dutifully executing some small domestic errand.
>
> Usually Malcolm was walking the dog (which
> made for much shorter, less satisfying conversations)
> going out to fetch something from a shop, or on his
> way to or from school/work.
>
> He was always eager to pass on the latest new bit of
> information he'd learned in school, and I was always
> eager to hear him out so we could launch into 20 minute
> conversation about one of our preferred topic areas.
>
> When I came away from most of those conversations
> was a vivid glimpse into Malcolm's personality … If I
> had to sum up Malcolm's personality in one word, based
> on our mutual exposure that word would be "Yes."
>
> Yes to being, to living, and to opening to the mys-
> tery of being human with all its ups and downs.
>
> He struck me as a very sensitive, thoughtful, deep-
> ly curious person, forward looking, with a particular

colour to that forward-looking momentum that I would have to call optimism.

I always got the sense that Malcolm's optimism came from an interior spiritual resource.

At times his visage appeared bright to me and I felt this brightness was akin to the reflections of brilliant sunlight off of the waves of a large deep body of water.

While the surface dances, hidden deep down below, a quiet, still place exists.

From Dr. D., more formally:

I have found it a great privilege to have gotten to know Malcolm in the ways I did. He was *such* a lovely person. Very principled and courageous, and gentle, and very rare to face a frightening illness and difficult medication decisions ... and all the while, he amazed me with his striking — and wonderfully absurd — sense of humour.

He was unusually insightful and intelligent, and very devoted to living a meaningful life. He also loved the two of you with great intensity, and often told me how loving and supportive you were to him and how lucky he was.

*

THE NIGHT OF the funeral Joe and Rebecca, Alison's niece and nephew, who had come from Victoria, British Columbia, left for home. The next day I made a late lunch of steak from the freezer for their mother Rosemary, and for Bill, who was also leaving. Alison and her sisters started to clean out Malcolm's room, the layers of the life he had left behind.

Layers, too, of people and their memories. We heard from them. From his childhood friend Holly in Scotsburn, Nova Scotia, with whom he watched TV and played on an Atari. From Celia, another Nova Scotian echo, and her son Duncan, who wrote, "It still brings a smile to my face to remember the time I was responsible for him and nearly had his eye put out with a [lawn] dart ... I'm sure I smile only because everything turned out okay but at the time I was petrified. My first close call."

And from his cousins, with whom he had so often consorted at Alison's clannish behest. They were the sons and daughters of her siblings: Polly, who had married a German immigrant; Rosemary, who married the son of Polish Jews; Liza, who married the son of Dutch immigrants. In his jocular way Alison's father liked to refer to his sons-in-law as "Fraser and the ethnics."

One of Alison's United Church colleagues recalled Malcolm as "gentle, funny, intelligent, wise, reflective, poetic." On their way back to Hamilton from the funeral she and her husband "saw a rainbow. The only one I've ever seen in the winter, especially on such a cold day." From Jerusalem one of the Bens who were his friends wrote that Malcolm was

a view of the world from a spiritual perspective
a desire to look beneath the surface and understand
the essence of things
a loving son who was proud of his family
fun fur gloves the face
a bright orange smile

He added, "I remember on a number of occasions dancing with Malcolm, he would pantomime a cellphone conversation with one hand, and wave his finger with the other, as if agreeing."

Addressing him by email, his Serbian friend Drazen recalled

the time we talked about the galaxies and the universe, you were the person who asked me the right questions about physics first. You wondered how the planets rotate, how the galaxies form, and where all the universe's energies came from.

We would go on tangents, but ultimately focus on the topic I know you were interested in the most. You mentioned life and reality are intertwined so that the energies flow from one medium to another. Like in a nuclear reaction, a gram of metal disappears into oblivion and is transformed into pure energy. Perhaps "Malcolm" is all that you weigh plus a few grams of your energies and thoughts.

I invited Malcolm's friends to pick what personal items they'd like to take as mementoes. On January 9 they sent him birthday greetings on Facebook. What I didn't hand over to his friends, and certainly didn't throw away, were the tidy or untidy piles of journals, notebooks, and college essays interspersed with colour sketches, diagrams, and energy-flow charts. On paper and in the computer he had faithfully recorded the results of his numerous esoteric experiments after the psychosis had hit him, what he was thinking and feeling. It was an archive of sorts.

*

I COULDN'T BEAR to share memories of Malcolm with Alison. To me they were excruciating shards of what had been lost. They were too painful to touch. To her they were something she wanted and needed to embrace. She shrieked at my unresponsiveness. Tottering into depression, she said she was no good to anyone and that I, everyone, would be better off without her. I knew we would be better off if she stopped drinking heavily.

∗

DAYS TAPERED INTO weeks, and weeks into months. We had dinner and absentmindedly set a place for Malcolm. We took the cakes to the homeless shelter and froze the soups and the casseroles. The bouquets died and we threw them out. We parcelled out mementoes to his friends. Shoes and clothes went to charity shops, Goodwill, or the Salvation Army. And there were lots of books: university texts, speculative fiction, and New Age. People continued to drop by, including two neighbour women I had never met. We put on smiling faces to meet their smiles.

The door to his room stayed open. There was now no reason for it to be closed. In the recent past Malcolm had spoken about moving out. From time to time it seemed about to happen. He wondered, in a mixture of caring and ego, about how it might affect us. Alison had told him first there had been three of us, and now there would be two. An obvious statement, but one with implications, a metaphor. Now she imagined he had just gone away, perhaps on a trip. For me, once the crowd of visitors had thinned, his absence was physical, a void that was also an ache, a hole that should have been be filled with him. He should have been behind a closed door.

Life became a matter of avoidance. I could not write anything, I could not read or view anything related to death or dead bodies, like the British TV series *Midsomer Murders*, which I used to watch on Monday nights. Malcolm would watch it with me, or watch me watching it. There in the living room he ought to have been lying on the couch, reading or with an eye on the TV. In the early morning, if the door of his room was ajar, I crept past in the hallway

29

lest I disturb him. Alison, who liked to walk around naked after a shower, would not have to take into account his repugnance, which she thought prudish, by calling out to him, "Naked mother coming!" In my office I would not hear him in the bathroom, getting ready for the day, the running water, the stir and shuffle, would not hear from him call as he left the house, "Bye, Dad."

As an extension of his absence for weeks I could not bear to write his name, or even his initial. The thought of writing a misery memoir about him seemed obscenely exploitative. To write *anything* about him seemed to betray the emotions I felt, at the very least it felt glib and inadequate. Even to touch the objects that belonged to him weighed down my hands, dishonoured his hands, the hands that had held and moved them.

No matter how much was cleared away, I found traces of him. A slip of paper with "Settings" written in his neat hand. A farm, a back road, a river bank, a waterfall, a lakeshore. In a canoe, in a tent. What did it mean? What could this list have been for — settings for a play? A video-game plot? It was almost a poem.

*

THE DYNAMIC OF marriage changed. The irritations and annoyances of three people living together was now a gap where a squabble used to be. Back then — recently, or was it long ago? — Alison specialized in walking away from me as she tossed back a remark or observation, and I did the same. Malcolm would be upstairs about to enter the bathroom when he'll shout down a statement or question and then close his door as if to foreclose a reply. A muffled voice might come from the depths of his room, but he might only be asking to me to bring him something, or to wake him up when, plainly, he was already awake. Both Alison and Malcolm would almost enter the room in which I was in but, rather than wait a moment to say what they were going to say in front of me, they'll utter it out in the hall. The habit of talking from a distance was contagious. The fact I was half deaf didn't help. As much as I deplored the practice, I did it, too. I'd come into the house and announce my presence, perhaps adding a profane comment about how cold it was, or about the success or failure of a shopping exped- ition. Sometimes, if we misjudged the situation in those days, words sounded in an empty house. I wondered why we did it. Was it be- cause we had something to say, and must say it instantly, regardless of whether anyone could hear it?

Often these utterances were only preliminaries in a chain of miscommunications. Alison or Malcolm would say something and I'd shout back, "WHAT?!" The distant statement might be repeat- ed, in the hope it would get through. More often it would be put in a slightly different form, so not only would the initial statement fail to be clear, but a second one would have to be deciphered. Additionally complicating the problem, the third person, seeking to be helpful, might choose to interpret or relay one or more of the preceding messages. Thus what had been an uncomprehending dialogue became a three-way exchange of ambiguous enquiries and misdirected pronouncements. This could go on for quite some time until, frustrated, distracted, or freshly occupied by something we'd engaged in or were about to do, we gave up. These charades, too, I missed.

One aversion the three of us shared was other people's loud- ness, especially from a family two doors up the street. When they gathered around their back-lawn inflatable pool, they yelled at each other so much we wondered that they didn't deafen each other like rock musicians. The kids shrieked, but their cries were lost in the adult exchanges. The adults, it was hard to tell which was which, would shout, "Pass the SALT!," "PASS the salt!," "The SALT!" When a party broke up, they shouted to departing visitors. Even the visitors were infected, shouting out the open windows of their cars as they drove away. The three of us listened like an alliance of the annoyed. These days, though, it was midwinter and the neighbours were silenced.

At home Malcolm had always been the conciliator, arbitrator, mediator, resolver of disputes. He was no longer there to do it. The absence of the problems he created, or his condition created for us, was an ongoing source of guilt at feeling relief at not having to take him into account. We would not have to take him into account in the ebb and flow of days. I would not have to worry that, when I was away on a trip or an extended errand, a psychotic event might reoccur, and I would not be there to deal with it. Even though it may have blocked or thwarted freedom of action, the problems were part of life's meaning, had added to a sense of self. At the same time they shrouded my future. I had often wondered how, gripped by psychosis, he would cope when I was gone.

In his absence, there was plenitude of a sort. Recording and sorting the pile of condolence cards, letters, and emails, the arrival of notices and tax forms, the messages from the public library: ("There are one or more items on hold for the customer with the initial M ... P ... S") the slow process of sorting and reshelving his books, the zoo or menagerie of stuffed animals heaped on top of a wardrobe in his room, brooding over what should be discarded and what should remain as welcome or burdensome links to the past. Alison asked whether I could ever bring myself to look through family photo albums. As yet I could not. But all I had to do was look around at the walls: those pictures in the living room of the three of us grinning seated on the back porch — twelve he would have been, eleven or twelve. Darcy, the champagne-coloured poodle we'd acquired in Nova Scotia who replaced Holly, the border collie, was grinning, too. A photo in the dining room: bearded, handsome, he didn't look like me, he didn't look like Alison. He looked like himself. I could not go to his Facebook page because I knew people had posted comments there, or to another website where a friend had posted some of his line drawings.

Was this what his life added up to, these reminders, to make this end? He had occupied twenty-six years of our lives. What was that all about? To put it at its most mundane, what had the $4,000 we paid an orthodontist for braces been about? He had been put into our keeping. A stranger withal, he resembled us in part. What he would become we didn't know, he was all becoming, not least in the way he grew apart from us. That part came into its own. We watched this stranger grow, grow taller, make friends, undergo glee and sorrow. When he wrapped himself in synthetic mysteries, magic, and the occult he became even more a stranger. From where, from whom would he get the answers he wanted? The trouble was — his trouble, our trouble — what he got were voices accusing him of unspeakable wrongs, wrongs for which he must atone.

I could hear his normal voice, but hearing it in my head didn't do me good and didn't do him good. He was dead. Alison would cry out, "I don't want to forget him!" As if remembering would bring him back, as if thinking what he said or did, or could say or do, could make him say and do. But was it about him at all? Was remembering the only proof that we lived with him for twenty-six years? Asking to remember only the good things, laughter and delight — what kind of life was that? Without the misery and craziness, a life half-lived. A "celebration of the life ..." That inane funeral formula. Thanks loads for having lived. Suppose we did remember everything, the joy and grief, the boredom and anxiety, what room was left for us to live, what was left for others to remember us by?

I told myself living with, experiencing someone, was a matter of the present. It wouldn't do to think of some earlier stage of a life — babyhood, toddlerhood, adolescence. That would be a pointless living in the past. Even less would it have been appropriate to consider only the future, that the only value he had was a potential for fulfillment — a conventionally successful career, a happy marriage, healthy children. One had to come to some kind of terms with him as he was any given moment.

In the first week, the first month, after his death, I behaved well, if behaving well meant going through stoical motions. Perhaps that was what a friend meant when he emailed that I had behaved with great dignity. Maybe, but Alison behaved heroically. She belied my fear she wouldn't. In earlier, lesser crises she sometimes had behaved less well or, like me, had just continued to function; at times she had crumbled, at others she seemed to needlessly anticipate or manufacture crises.

Now the extent of her heroism was measured by what she didn't do. She could have drunk herself into oblivion, embarrassing herself and possibly others, though I supposed they would have understood. But, despite having quit Alcoholics Anonymous, which she had joined six years earlier, she didn't embark on a binge. She could have flailed at someone's incautious remarks. She did in fact do that once, when her sister Polly begged her not to drink "for my sake," but that only happened once. Nearly all the time she was poised, welcoming, receptive to others' pain, only retreating when exhaustion dragged her to bed early. Having to make up for the time she had taken off from work, she returned to it, surprised and relieved that her boss, who had zero managerial skills, was nicer to her.

Malcolm's death seemed inseparable from his illness, almost as if the illness had been a kind of death, or at least its preliminary. I kept remembering its low points, its twists and turns, its individual separate griefs. When the depth and extent of that illness had become obvious, I had said to Alison, she remembered, "Our lives are over." She had wisely replied that that part of our life was over. Something else had begun, but we had no idea of what its shape and duration would be.

Weeks after he died, I had my first dream about him. It was his birthday and he was opening presents. I remembered I'd been so busy I'd forgotten to get him a present. Then I thought I'd just give him $50 to buy what he wanted. In the dream I got the feeling that would be all right with him.

Three months after he died I was out of the country for a week. While I was away, Alison had her own dream about him. In one, he appeared and she said, "But I thought you were dead." He said, "Yes, I am." "Can I give you a hug?" "Sure." She hugged him. She asked him whether he was in heaven. He said he was and she asked him what it was like. He said he didn't want to talk about it.

In another dream, she saw him washing dishes in the kitchen, which I usually did. She asked why he was doing it. He said, "Oh, I just wanted to help out." Then the dream shifted and I was blaming her for not telling my brother how seriously ill Malcolm was, which was why he hadn't come to see us in Toronto.

*

AMONG OUR EXPORTS from Nova Scotia was parti-coloured Becky. Becky, whom I usually described as a "hideous Nova Scotian barn cat" had always been Malcolm's favourite. I often thought of her, full of complaints, as the reincarnation of my mother. One mild morning she wanted out. I opened the back door for her. By the end of the day she had not returned. This worried me, not because I was attached to her, but because Alison and Malcolm were, especially Malcolm. They sometimes accused me of neglecting her. I would be eating dinner off a tray in the living room and toss a morsel to Barnaby. Becky prepared to pounce on it. I pushed her away with my foot. "Daa-add!" Malcolm cried out indignantly. I protested that Becky regularly stole meals from Barnaby. "Then go and get something for her!" Alison snapped. I said I now knew my position in the family pecking order: it was lower than the cat.

I knew that I would be affected by the loss of her, if it proved to be one, because Becky carried within her tattered skinny greedy body the body of the past. Born in a barn, patrolling in the open air, air-freighted to the city, she was like a senile war veteran to be honoured, not because she had fought in a distinguished cause, but by virtue of still being around. She used our next-door neighbour Therese's house as a dosshouse until we would get a phone call to fetch her.

More than twenty years old — about a hundred in human years? — she had grown skeletal in the past year, a furry bundle of bones, sometimes wetting the carpet. She had always been greedy, given to gobbling Barnaby's meals, but now she was ravenous. For some time I had thought of taking her to the veterinarian to be put down, an ongoing source of anxiety for Malcolm. I procrastinated, hoping natural causes would intervene. That day she did not drag herself home. We never saw her again.

*

ALISON WANTED TO talk to someone about Malcolm, talk to anyone, to as many people as possible. Most of all she wanted to talk to me about him. I wondered if that would make her feel better or worse. I wondered whether, just as expressing anger can make you angrier, expressing grief might make you grieve all the more. For me, everything was either a distraction or a painkiller. But Malcolm was always the subtext. Every so often I would be ambushed by grief. Yet sometimes I wondered if, day-to-day, I was really unhappier than I usually was due to ordinary lifetime mix of anxieties, neuroses, hypochondria, depression, and torpor.

For Alison, the third week after his death seemed to be the worst. She felt constantly shivery and nauseous, as if she had the flu.

I came home late one afternoon to find her disoriented, panicking she'd forgotten what day of the week it was. "Is it Tuesday?" I worried she might be having a stroke. I heard sounds down the hall. She was in the bathroom, sobbing. "Malcolm's *dead*," she said. That angered me. "I'm aware of that," I said. I could not enter her thicket of shared memories. She bitterly resented that. I had failed her.

*

THREE MONTHS AFTER Malcolm's death I got an email from Kulu, Valley of the Gods, India, where Monique, the Frenchwoman I had lived with in Montreal, lived in the Meditation Centre of Swami Shyam, a sane and unexploitative guru. She now called herself Chataiya. Frailer, her health beginning to fail, she wrote me, "The heart has no frontiers, no time, and so very few words."

She had come to see us in Toronto when Malcolm was fourteen. Alison had suggested he and Monique go into the garden and talk in French, but they switched slowly to English, covering metaphysics, India, and meditation. Years later, when she visited again, he had become taller, a handsome lively humorous young man. She thought he was still searching for something he knew was in himself but could not reach. He had started to meditate a lot. She sensed he loved the pure silence, something university courses could not give him. He was, she thought, deep in his own consciousness of the real truth. Maybe that was just her wishful thinking. I had the uneasy feeling that all the meditation he did had been somehow unhealthy.

*

IN LATE MAY, Alison wrote "a poem or something." She'd always been diffident about writing verse, usurping my status, pretending to be a professional, rather as if I were a medical doctor and she presumed to hand out prescriptions. What she wrote now tracked her grief over time, and how grief inflected everything she saw and heard. The editor in me wanted to revise the poems. But that was pointless. They were hers.

She wrote how we had sex for the first time since his death. The conjugal act was satisfactory, she concluded, not bad for people in their sixties, each with an inconvenient medical condition (which one did she mean?) and after thirty-some years of marriage.

She wrote how she'd rise from the couch and flee to the bathroom to weep, bawling like a cow who had lost her calf. Every song she heard seemed to have "remember" in it. A young man came into a subway car with peace and purpose in his face. Even a gang of obnoxious teenagers filled her with delight. Ashley, one of Malcolm's best friends, brought her flowers on Mothers' Day.

She was grateful for it, everyone's memories of him. She was grateful for her own crowd of memories. She was grateful to be left alone. She was resentful and contemptuous and demanding. She behaved beautifully and comforted the comforters. Their loss completed her own.

She wrote how, after the funeral, we went through his room again, giving away, donating, and discarding. Things he kept "for sentimental reasons," he used to tell us with a glint in his eye when we urged him to throw them out. T-shirts from jobs — security firms, restaurants, city recreation. Exasperating (to his mother) New Age books beside the King James Bible and *Choose Your Own Adventure.* All his academic papers, sketch books, jewelry he made, stuffed toys. Love letters from a girlfriend, CDs from music festivals, the residue of Christmas stockings, a battery-operated piggy bank.

So much started and left unfinished, journals begun but mainly filled with pages never to be written on. So much self-delusion, dreams outgrown, dreams he abandoned, so much triumph, all with the extra dimension he gave everything. And so much dust.

She saw a young woman glowing with what she deemed to be a joyful pregnancy and it reduced her to helpless tears. It was not so much wanting grandchildren of her own, it was more that life went on without him.

Jokes we could not share with him, anecdotes about the cats, movies coming out he would have liked, a production of *As You Like It* they might have gone to. That we seldom saw her nieces and nephews, that they didn't answer emails. That life was moving on. She hoped that young woman would be happy with her child, that she would have the laughter that we did and, yes, the pain. So much started and not finished, so much self-delusion. So much everything.

As late as July poems of a sort were still coming to her. For an instant, for a heartbeat, she was holding Malcolm's body in her arms, keening. "He's better off dead," she thought aloud, "At least we don't need to worry about him now." She recalled that he asked, "Will I ever feel healthy again?" They had spoken of those with disabilities and imperfections, and how this described us all. "Did I bring this on myself?" he asked.

*

ABOUT THIS TIME we got the prose of the coroner's report. The autopsy didn't tell us much, though it had taken nearly eight months to reach its conclusions. Coronary arteries and cardiac valves: "Unremarkable." Neck and respiratory system: Unremarkable. Digestive system: Unremarkable. Genitourinary System, Head and Central Nervous System, Other Organs and Tissues — all of them Unremarkable. The stomach contents, barley and mushroom — something I made for dinner, a concession to his vegetarianism.

So why was he dead? "Cause of Death: Sudden Unexpected Death in Epilepsy." He'd never had epileptic fits, so I supposed epilepsy was just the vague general term applied to people who'd died as he did.

Malcolm, the report said,

> had a six-year history of schizophrenia and had reportedly used illicit drugs when younger. He was currently on psychiatric medications including clozapine, respiridone, and cogentin. Ten days before death, he experienced his first seizure. MRI was negative. He was said to be well the evening before he was found dead in bed. He had been using ibuprofen for back pain following the seizure, which was changed to Tylenol #3.
>
> Post mortem examination revealed no anatomical cause of death. Specifically, there was no evidence of significant injury or natural disease....
>
> Toxicological analysis of post mortem blood showed only a therapeutic concentration of clozapine. There was no evidence of toxic levels of any drug or poison.
>
> Death is attributed to sudden unexpected death in epilepsy (SUDEP), where people with epileptic seizures die unexpectedly without a clear cause of death.

That was our answer.

*

WE LEARNED THAT Daniel, the twenty-three-year-old son of one of her cousins, who lived in a town southwest of the city, had hanged himself. An uncle had done the same thing many years before. After

Malcolm's death Dan had written on Facebook that "we are all much poorer not having you here." It had become his turn.

The next day we drove to the pretty town of Elora for Dan's outdoor funeral. We sang "Lean on Me." Following it Alison, pained by an infected tooth, got drunk on vodka. Weeping and furious, she felt she had been excluded when her sisters gathered in nearby Acton, ostensibly conferring about the welfare of their brother Rob. When Rosemary arrived from Victoria she shouted at her over the phone, then apologized. At the same time, she was ashamed of herself for her obsession with her sisters, compared to the death of our son. "What does it *matter*?" she says. I made her lie down. Later she walked with me to the liquor store to buy Scotch. By now *I* needed a drink.

Suicide and suicide attempts ran like a ragged crimson thread in her family. Alison's paternal grandmother had died by suicide, her father had attempted it, and before we married she had, too — several times. We saw Dan annually at family gatherings, as glowingly handsome and intelligent as Malcolm. We had heard he had dropped out of college. The previous August his brother had discovered him trying to kill himself. With Malcolm's room vacant we had discussed whether we might offer it to him, at least invite him over for a meal. But did we want another disturbed young man around? We were still mulling over the idea when we learned he was living with his brother in the city's west end, and decided not to interfere with the family's arrangements. We had last seen him at a little party we'd given for Alison's sister Rosemary from Victoria. He looked cheerful and humorous.

The day we learned of his death Eva, our Polish cleaning lady, was tidying our bedroom. Knowing she was jumpy, Malcolm used to creep up behind her to say, "Boo!" This day she heard a thump behind her. As usual, she jumped. Now a Bible, fallen off a shelf, lay open on the floor. She thought it must be Malcolm, sending her a message. She reproached herself for not checking the passage that had been exposed. Hearing about the incident, a friend of Malcolm said, grinning, "If Malcolm did come back from the other side it would have been to mess up somebody's mind."

PART TWO

MALCOLM WAS BORN on January 11, 1984. He was conceived in Nelson, a hillside town in the British Columbia interior, where I'd been teaching writing, so-called, at a junior college. Because of the arts-hating provincial government's budget cutbacks I lost my job. Driving our aged Toyota cross-country, we were in downtown Toronto by July.

By late December Alison began to look like a corpulent stork: huge belly, stick legs. For months, elderly Italian men on the Queen Street streetcar had patted her belly for good luck. A flickering screen had shown a baby with a thumping heart. At the turn of the year her mucus plug had broken — apparently a good thing — and she felt her much-anticipated first contraction. Dr. P., a Women's College Hospital obstetrician, a burly, bearded man, had gravely warned us not to follow the current vogue of having babies delivered underwater. Perhaps we seemed like people who would favour that kind of thing. But having our son — and it was going to be a son — born underwater was not something we had contemplated. We did want everything to transpire as naturally as possible.

We had to sign waivers of legal responsibility in declining two routine invasive procedures: we did not want him circumcised, nor did we want him to undergo another kind of pain — silver nitrate drops in his eyes. The drops were prescribed by an old law that apparently assumed every new mother had gonorrhea.

We faithfully attended Lamaze lessons and prenatal classes at the mainly female-patient Women's College Hospital, joining the pretended contractions of sitting and stretching expectant mothers and their mates. Now, on January 10, the real contractions were under way. Apart from consulting the Canada geese during strolls along the nearby shore of Lake Ontario, we'd spent the day timing them: at first twenty minutes apart, eventually four minutes apart. A doctor subbing for Dr. P. told us to come in. At midnight a friend drove us to the hospital.

The friend's wife had once said sardonically about childbirth, "First you do your breathing exercises and then you call for major drugs." As my friend drove us to the hospital I continued the circular massage with the palm of my hand I'd started hours earlier — effleurage, it was called. But it did little to ease the pains. Once we got there Alison became obsessed with registering her contractions. About 4:00 a.m. I dozed off for about twenty minutes in a corner armchair. When I woke up, Alison was desperate with pain, counting in a spooky, spacey voice, "One, two, three, four, five, six, seven, eight …" Since we were determined to be noninvasive, to do everything the natural way, we'd forsworn an amniotomy (puncturing the amniotic sac) and an epidural (injecting a numbing medicine in the space around the spinal nerves in the lower back). But we hadn't counted on this much pain. A young, fast-talking Italian resident said Alison should have an amniotomy and epidural. We yielded. A surgeon punctured the sac with what looked like a long, plastic, barbed ruler and, with a catheter, put an electronic monitor on the baby's skull. So much for natural methods.

After twenty minutes she had no more pain. We dozed off for about an hour. By now it was past seven. She was pronounced ready to go. A middle-aged lady who'd been quietly competent all night was succeeded by a young, chubby, wide-faced woman, a slave driver. She shouted, "Push, push, push that baby out!"

Dr. P., who had been home looking after a sick son, arrived. He said Alison should go to the delivery room at nine or so. The baby's head was off to the side a bit, apparently. More pushing while I supported Alison's shoulders and pushed with her, sweat running off my face. At nine she was wheeled off.

I was pacing near the nursing station when someone told me she was in the delivery room. I grabbed a green surgical gown and cap. A roadblock of doctors and nurses wouldn't allow me into the room until they reached Dr. P. for permission. That acquired, the anaesthetist, a Mitteleuropean lady, took me in. I stood at the head of the bed. Alison's legs were in stirrups. What I saw next should have reminded me of calves being born back on my father's farm, but didn't. Dr. P. appeared and more stuff was pulsed through the epidural. Alison was made to push more. I watched in the mirror as Dr. P. levered a flat, saddle-like forceps into her vagina, turning the baby around. Then the head emerged, greyish through the bloody wound. With what looked like a scoop in his hands, Dr. P. eased out our son's head, then the rest of him, cut the umbilical cord, wiped blood away. Eerily, there had been no sound when the baby, the whole baby, emerged face down. He began to cry, but not compulsively or especially loudly. He seemed almost content to be in the world.

"Can I hold him?" Alison said pathetically, almost melodramat- ically, after they'd cut the umbilical cord, wiped blood away.

"He's perfect," I said to myself in wonder and surprise. Physically perfect. Given our family histories, it seemed miracu- lous he was. Alison was thirty-eight; she had miscarried two years earlier while we'd been in Paris briefly, and we'd had a scare during a visit to Nova Scotia when she began bleeding, but it had been a false alarm — a cervical polyp.

He was physically perfect. Not like Alison's brother Rob, born microcephalic ("pinheaded," people used to say), Alison's overweight, shambling brother nervously stumbling over his words. Not like Hughie, my five-years-older brother born with severe cerebral palsy due to my parents' Rh blood incompatibility, the same factor that had led to my being rushed to a faraway hospital for a total blood transfusion as an infant. Hughie couldn't read, write, speak, or sit up, much less walk or feed himself. Hence the ungodly toil my mother endured for many years, only a small part of which she could delegate to me. I had to hold an empty tin can for Hughie to pee into; as it happened, a can that had once held peas. That I could do anything to help was natural; after all, I was perforce the girl of the family.

An intermission. They took Malcolm away to test his heart rate and muscle tone, his Apgar score. The score's top was ten, Malcolm's was nine. He weighed eight pounds, eight ounces.

Alison was very happy but very pale, shuddering with cold. Dr. P. congratulated us, pro forma. They washed the baby and we went off to a recovery room, then to a four-bed ward.

We were going to call him Malcolm Patrick. His first name had no negative connotations for us, and I whimsically mused that, like his namesake in *Macbeth*, he would recover his father's kingdom — not that I had any kingdom to speak of. His second name was that of his maternal grandmother's adored brother, who had died in a training accident during the Second World War.

I was utterly whacked. Before I left the hospital I saw my son in the nursery incubator where his temperature was being stabilized. He was delicate, perfect.

Early afternoon I took a taxi home, thinking these lines:

> *May I be a better father than my father*
> *May you be a better son than his son*

I sent out cards to friends and relations:

FRASER & ALISON SUTHERLAND
ARE PLEASED TO ANNOUNCE
THE BIRTH OF A SON
MALCOLM PATRICK
11 JAN. 1984 TORONTO, CANADA.

Congratulations Preferred

In return came a cascade of stork, flower, and baby-bunting greeting cards.

*

OUR APARTMENT WAS in Parkdale, a west-end neighbourhood of once-gracious Victorian homes that had declined economically over the decades to a place where Indians and Pakistanis seeking affordable rents intermingled with panhandlers, street people, and chemically stilled psychiatric patients outplaced from institutions. It was upstairs from the office of a Serbian dentist and his wife, who owned the small building and strangely seemed happy to rent the apartment to an underemployed writer and his pregnant wife. We changed diapers on a folding table in the narrow hall; Malcolm spent most of his days in a tall, slatted crib in the little living room overlooking the busy street.

Alison and I had contrived a hopeful list of division-of-labour appointed tasks, allocating cookery, shopping, and laundry to me, and to Alison folding, ironing, putting washed and dried clothes away, as well as bedmaking, vacuuming (once a week), tidying, and dishwashing. Ah yes, the baby. Baby care was theoretically divided between us.

Feeding, changing, bathing him. Alison was encouraged, we wrote in our self-memo, to take a time-off break from the apartment. We resolved to free one night a week so we could go out together. Sure, sure.

As if to give myself time off, or just to shun work, I came down with the flu — chills, fever, nausea — while Alison segued into bottle-feeding, which she described as like "pouring milk down a sump-hole."

Malcolm went to sleep after stormy squalls, varied by cries in the night, keeping Alison unpredictably awake with demands for meals. She gazed down at him as he fed. She said she had the theory that "babies put down and left get eaten by pye dogs or jackals." She occasionally resorted to the old-fashioned remedy of whisky tot, sugar, and water to get him to sleep. When I got up in the morning I'd find notes that began, "The wretched child woke at 3:00 a.m. & went hard till 7." She warned me not to wake her up, adding, "Might be less annoying if he were less charming. About 5:30 he gave me a lovely seraphic smile. 'Isn't this *nice*, mum? Just you & me, all nice & peaceful. But so interesting & stimulating! I *am* enjoying this.'"

*

PULLING ASIDE THE thick ruby velveteen curtains, I saw it was still dark outside, chilly mist swirling around the streetlamps. I couldn't see the cars except for their piercing lights. When darkness lifted, I could see Malcolm in his crib, tiny, plump. His grin lit the room as he gripped the crib slats, a pillar of light, a mild torch, in the smudge of our lives.

No less negligent than many fathers, I did my best to dodge what Alison encouragingly, optimistically, but unconvincingly called "all the fun" of baby care, the diaper-changing, the spoon-feeding after he had progressed from breast to bottle to dribbled purées. Alison wasn't having any shirking of shared childcare; in fact, she seemed to resent the fact I wasn't lactating.

In one of the snapshots we took I am bottle-feeding Malcolm from a bottle of milk that Alison had expressed, the nipple in his mouth, the bottle propped under my chin. Sometimes I varied the performance with a head-fake in order to persuade him I was a breast. He would unavailingly strive to summon forth milk. Alison's mother Althea said I was the only man she'd ever met who knew how to tease a month-old baby.

With a finer sense of family obligations than I had, Alison flew Malcolm east to Nova Scotia so his grandparents could meet him. Since in our late thirties it was improbable we were going to have another child, and my long-divorced brother showed no inclination to remarry, much less become a father, Malcolm was likely the only grandchild they would ever know, the end of a Sutherland bloodline.

A photo in shades of grey commemorates the meeting of grandfather and new grandson. In a hospital bed my father holds Malcolm in his lap, looking down and away from him. I read unposed tenderness in his face. Presumably, he had long given up any prospect of a grandchild. It was difficult to know whether satisfaction or pleasure was what he felt, or whether he resented being forced into a photograph ceremonial. Advanced age had reached him and he was ailing. At any age he had never been one to betray feelings.

In Toronto there was another grandparent, Alison's widowed mother. Althea had four daughters and a son, all except Rosemary in Victoria more or less in proximity. Malcolm had several cousins of roughly the same age. An implicit vigil surrounded Althea. She had been diagnosed with pancreatic cancer, and the odds of her survival were low. We had lived with her for a few months in the big house of her widowhood when we had returned from British Columbia. I thought she would have liked us to stay, perhaps to assuage loneliness. But we had wanted our own untidy nest. When Malcolm was born, Alison expected from her the rapture that had attended the arrival of previous grandchildren, but it didn't come. She was noncommittal. When Alison tearfully protested at the seeming indifference, she said, "Everything's ashes."

*

FROM THE PARKDALE apartment I would set off with Malcolm bundled papoose style into a Snugli baby carrier bound to my chest. I used these marsupial outings to buy snacks from a Pakistani take-out or a Polish deli, and the two of us would come back encrusted with chickpea and pastry crumbs.

Within the bounds of the apartment Malcolm gave vent to utterances, as if dictating them. "Urgh!," "Woo wah!," "Naweeoba!," "Unblsglah!" Alison duly tabulated them. She also got him to pound my computer keyboard keys, calling the result "Malcolm's first poem."

The demands of an imperious baby, an emperor only son, dominated domestic life. In the evenings, half ashamed of myself, I was depressed by what seemed to be Alison's non-stop obsession with Malcolm. Where once she and I had taken account of each other's wants, needs, demands, and responses came interventions from a third party. As a tribute to Sigmund Freud, I began to protest what seemed to me unduly prolonged breast-feeding and obsessive mothering. "You have three topics morning, noon, and night," I told Alison. "(1) Malcolm, (2) Malcolm, (3) Malcolm. I don't want to be (2) or (3); I'd just be grateful if *anything* would."

The little apartment turned claustrophobic. We needed a break, I thought, at least for one evening. Hiring a babysitter, we saw the documentary film *Seven-Up*, the first of a series in which British youngsters are followed through seven-year sequences of their lives. It was an outstanding documentary, but we were restless to get back to the apartment. We'd taken a temporary respite.

Since Alison and I both had jobs, we eventually took on a string of babysitters, augmented by Althea and by Alison's available sisters. They oversaw his transition from breast to bottle (which might hold everything from Alison's manually expressed milk to formula to goat's milk) then to Pablum and puréed carrots, and introduced him to a walker, a swing, and the Jolly Jumper apparatus, its harness suspended from a door frame. They didn't always have it easy. He'd been a fidgety and cranky eater. Alison gave babysitters detailed notes about baby care and insisted they keep a log, which they faithfully did: "10:55–11:45. Laid him down for a nap. He fussed for about 5 minutes. I went in and rubbed his back & he fell right to sleep." Alison replied, "Good! I never tried that! Wonder if it would work for me!"

Once Malcolm became ambulatory I'd take him across the street to a wok-and-noodle takeout, where we'd sit waiting for our order. Suddenly he wasn't there. Even in the fits of absent-mindedness to which I was sometimes subject, I couldn't imagine he'd exited through the front door. Panic rose in me. Then the kitchen door swung open and a grinning Chinese cook surfaced, holding him by the hand.

Parkdale was living up to Toronto's smug self-image as a multiculture. Among our hired help was a comely and competent young Filipina at whom I directed covert lascivious glances, and a sad-eyed, gentle Egyptian Copt. Lastingly, a large voluble young woman, this time white, named Chris, who supplemented her welfare payments with childcare. She had the habit of dropping cigarette ashes on her charges. This didn't bother Alison unduly, because Althea had done the same thing. Supplementing our lake-front walks (we imagined Malcolm's saying, "Quite something, those gulls, ducks, and geese"), Chris often took Malcolm back to her own place, an erratic boyfriend sometimes present, or she'd go on lengthy, unscheduled expeditions with them both, or just with Malcolm. But in her careless bountiful way she was tactile and affectionate, which outweighed her waywardness.

Alison's trip to Nova Scotia had been timely, because soon afterward my father died. I went east for the funeral, and to be with my mother in her first days of widowhood. In the big house on the sloping, leafy Toronto street, Althea, weakening from pancreatic cancer, losing weight she could not afford to lose, her face yellowed with jaundice, was sinking fast. Always brave, stoical, she did not protest when we said we would spend Christmas with my widowed mother. She thought it was the right thing to do. She was a woman who always wanted to do the right thing. When we got to Nova Scotia, anxious phone calls flew between Alison and her sisters keeping a watch on their mother. Between unhappy Christmas and unhappy New Year's Althea died. Alison flew back with Malcolm to the funeral.

*

WE MOVED, CHRIS the babysitter migrating with us to Althea's big, empty house. The residential stretch of ersatz castles and tall maples plunged down the hill before untangling itself from other gracious streets. Cars used it as a shortcut to downtown, flattening squirrels. There were no sidewalks.

The walls of the dim rooms were painted a becoming shade of mustard, a single light bulb gaped in a dining-room chandelier. Outside, a stone owl presided over the property like a placating deity. Clematis climbed a gazebo, its roof layered with grapevines. A trellis for rambler roses was nailed at the back of the stoop the family called "the Admiral's Walk." Down rough stone steps from the bottom of the garden, past wild trilliums, a huge wedge of tree at the bottom had crashed during the winter, crushing the fence of the ravine park here. One day within this sloping wilderness Malcolm stumbled, gashing his forehead on the stub of a fallen branch. We rushed him to a hospital where, tied to a bed, pale and frightened, he was stitched up. He would have a small scar above an eyebrow, like the one I bore from a childhood tumble.

*

FOR HALLOWEEN HE was costumed as a wolf. He ran in circles as fast as his little legs could carry him, crying, "I'm a wolf! I'm a wolf!" He made the transition from the imaginative to the literal later, when he started playing with that mysterious device, the telephone, dialing numbers at random. One day Alison came upon him speaking into its mouthpiece, very irritated.

"What do you *mean*, hang up and try my call again?"

*

ALISON HAD A steady job at a downtown public library. We could perhaps have mustered the down payment for Althea's house, but some factors militated against it. It was much too large for us, and in a neighbourhood far above our station. And it might not have sat well with Alison's sisters. They might have felt they were forced by moral suasion to give us a break on the price. Real-estate prices were starting to soar. We could imagine how her siblings would feel if, greedily turning a quick profit, we flipped Althea's home. Besides, a familiar gravitation tugged me to Nova Scotia again (in my entire life I had never missed a Christmas), and to another big house. But this was the one in which my mother lived alone on the non-working farm she and my father acquired not long before I began my teens. She would come to know her grandson. Mom to me, Mary to everyone else, she would be Granny to him. How the four of us would get on I didn't know.

In Toronto the home of Alison's youth was put up for sale. It quickly went to a wealthy brewer's wife. The silverware, furnishings, heirlooms, and all the china, china, china got tensely divided among the daughters. We put out by the curb a rusty bedspring, a crumpled mattress, and broken furniture. In the morning everything was gone.

*

THE RURAL NEIGHBOURHOOD to which we migrated was called Hardwood Hill, on a few curves of the narrow highway east of the village of Scotsburn. Mom's white-porched sprawling farmhouse stood at the top of the hill up a gully-prone lane. On one side of the icebound front yard was a big red disused barn. Looming above the snowy lawn, leafless elms and maples leaned. Winter had begun in Toronto, but it was colder here.

After a preliminary visit a few months earlier we arrived in mid-November, a week ahead of our goods, which were conveyed in an eighteen-wheeler by a chain-smoking, alcoholic, cowboy-booted driver. By the driver's numbering system we were missing two cartons, by mine we were missing one. However, it, or they, turned up. A pity. I'd put on lots of insurance.

*

ALISON LEARNED LOCAL folkways: e.g., how to respond to the characteristic phone greeting "Hi!" (spoken with a grunting out-take of breath, much like the "How!" of an old Western, without further identification). One day a neighbour woman reported a fire in her son's garage by screaming down the telephone line, "Hi! Hi! Hi! Hi!" Malcolm picked up Mom's idiom about television. "There's my program!" she would announce, or "My program's on!" He did likewise. She also took note of his imaginative powers; toys or anything like a machine were of little use to him. Becoming impatient at having things done for him, he developed his own catchphrases: "That's not nice!" and "That's not fair!" and "That's not a nice thing to say." When I, Mom, or Alison shouted at each other, he would say, "Wait a minute, guys."

Alison gained eleven pounds and was a mere self of her former shadow. Solidifying her community credentials and capitalizing on the five years of religious life she'd had in the past, on Christmas Eve she sang in Scotsburn's Bethel Presbyterian Church choir. Later became Sunday School Superintendent.

In one way she was still in Toronto, since she was in frequent communication with her sisters there, usually about the welfare of their brother. Let a = Alison in Nova Scotia, and b, c, and d = her sisters in Toronto, Peterborough, and Victoria. A typical exchange might entail a telling b what c is doing, confirming to c that d told b about a, and so on. Mom, when not on the telephone going "Hi!," attended to the gelded ginger tomcat Travis, which she'd long boarded for us. "Where's the cat? Did you put the cat outside?" "Is that cat in the pantry?" "Is that old bugger upstairs?" Mom, seventy-eight, on the subject of teenage promiscuity: "Jumping Judas! Young people today can't do anything except be jazzing around every night. Before I'd do that, I'd go out and shoot myself."

Holly, Mom's madly manic border collie, regarded everything as a sheep: Malcolm, visiting children, my foot, the cat, etc., staring hypnotically at them, then at the merest motion diving in to herd. When Travis did his daily laundry you could see Holly thinking: "What's a sheep doing washing its face?"

On New Year's Eve Alison and I took in a party in the woods where hippies were reconstructing themselves into yuppies. There were many children underfoot. Mothers and fathers would clutch the latter to their bosoms in poses suitable for reproduction in a book entitled, say, *Parenting: The Loving Way.*

We showed Malcolm, turning three, a picture of a rhino in a book. We asked him, "What's that?" and he responded, "I don't know. A bear!" Before going out to have a meal at a diner he told us, "Yukky restaurants make me unhappy. Clean restaurants make me happy." The statement would have carried more conviction if he had not climbed into the next cubicle and started to guzzle a bottle of ketchup.

During breakfast at home he and Granny dialogued. Malcolm is eating a boiled egg, Travis hovering nearby. Malcolm says, "Granny, you make good eggs." Mom (pretending to be Travis), would reply, "I can eat an egg." Holding out a spoonful of boiled egg, Malcolm says, "Come here, Travie, I will give you some." Granny: "No, no, no, no." Malcolm: "Well, OK. You can have a fried egg." Fried eggs were favourites. To Granny he'd say of one she gave him, "Nice and soft, mmm, thank you, Granny — mighty tasty!"

Occasionally he'd have a row with Granny. He would hurl a spoon at her, she would hurl it back. Malcolm went purple with rage, very funny. Adults kept giggling, Malcolm got angrier and angrier. "Stop laughing at me!" Mom watched him while he messed about with aluminum pie plates on the floor near the kitchen sink, replicating what I had reportedly done as a toddler when I demanded to "play in the pink."

Mom was concerned Malcolm didn't see Alison naked, presumably because it might later lead to teenage promiscuity. It was just as well she never heard Alison explaining the use of Tampax. One day he announced, "When I grow up, I'm going to be a girl." I said, "OK, Malcolm, we'll make an appointment to see the doctor. If you want to be a girl, you'll have to have an operation and have your balls cut off." Malcolm thought for a moment, and said, "No, I'm going to be a girl and *keep* my balls."

When rebuked for spilling an ashtray, he said, "Oh well, these things happen." Those first years he was besotted with his fuzzy blanket. Alison reflected on how lovely it was to have something in one's life as sensuously and psychologically satisfying as fuzzy blankets were to Malcolm. Walking down the lane to the mailbox with her, he no longer asked her to carry him. He pretended he had picked her up and carried *her* most tenderly, assuring her he wouldn't let her fall. Helping Malcolm out of his bath, she held the edge of a towel in her teeth. Malcolm cried, "Don't put the towel in your mouth — you might swallow it!" He had concern for others. When he was at a playgroup and bouts of tears came from other children, he at once stopped playing and went over to see what the matter was, offering cookies.

Meanwhile, I spent my time trying to revise the unpublishable, and to publish the unrevisable.

Sometimes I morbidly thought the words I gave Malcolm for grace at meals and bed-time prayers were all that would survive of me, even though what I taught him to say would rely more on hope than on faith. The words Mom had taught me to say at night when I was his age:

> *Now at last I lay my head*
> *For rest and dreams inside my bed*
> *God shall help me through the night*

And shall make the morning bright
But just before I go to sleep
I ask him please to bless and keep.

She had made me add a line about my cerebral-palsied brother.

Make Hughie well

and, naturally,

Make Fraser a good boy

but this time not I, but my son, was to respond:

God bless Mummy, God bless Daddy,
God bless everybody else in the whole world.

Already these words were pro forma, though, sentimentally, I thought one day he might teach them to his own children, at his own table say the grace I composed, nicely ecumenical — both Marxist atheists and believing Christians could repeat it without wincing:

For good things we have let us be thankful.
May we always share each of our blessings.

*

WITH A LITTLE money in hand, I wanted the sun. Even before we moved in with Mom, we had settled on a holiday in Portugal. Why Portugal? My stock answer: "It's warm, it's cheap, and there's lots of fish to eat — even if they are caught off Newfoundland."

En route, we paused in London, where we stayed in Ham Common, in the motherhouse of the Community of the Sisters of the Church, an Anglican order founded in the late nineteenth century under the patronage of St. Michael and All Angels. A former novice there, Alison had friends and a few enemies among the hundred or so Sisters scattered all the way from the United Kingdom to Canada, Australia, and the Solomon Islands. One became a full Sister in stages: aspirant, novice, junior sister, and finally taker of life vows. Alison had spent five years as a novice. The Sisters took Malcolm in their smiling stride. They gave him rides around the refectory on the food trolley, making train noises.

Alison thought he was going to have a very peculiar idea of what the religious life was all about.

At dinner Judith, the Australia-born Mother Superior, caused Malcolm's brow to furrow when she said to Malcolm, "Just think, if Alison stayed with us Fraser wouldn't be here and Malcolm wouldn't be here." Malcolm's face dropped. What! Me not here?!"

I took my leave to scout for somewhere in Portugal we could live pleasantly for two months. I settled on the small, tuna-fishing port of Tavira, west of the Algarve. Alison and Malcolm arrived at Lisbon airport. From the baggage terminal Malcolm grinned from atop a trolley, rejoicing in the ride.

In Tavira an amused welcoming soul with a wide face and thick black hair like a sturdy peasant, perhaps inevitably called Maria, housed us for the night and found us a clean, airy apartment amid the novelty of oranges and limes actually growing on trees, ripening and dropping. The grounds seemed to specialize in snails. Portugal was the world's biggest supplier of carob pods, sometimes used in cookies and as a coffee substitute. I grew tired of lugging a three-year-old around town on my shoulders. I thought he could have used his own feet more, especially since he could scale a sprawling lowslung carob tree. Malcolm didn't drink coffee but he got alternative treats. Middle-aged men made it a habit to hand out candies to children his age and he got his share.

Sometimes verse again overtook Alison. About Malcolm she reflected:

> You do much for me —
> > teach me how much I can endure — I can endure
> > infinitely, it seems
> You teach me fearless, guiltless anger
> You teach me slowness,
> > peace, fascination for the microscopic....
> You are my gift to yourself,
> My gift to the world
> I want, honestly, nothing of you for myself
> And yet you give yourself to me, prodigiously,
> > > insistently
> > > imperiously
> And from me launch yourself
> Generously, furiously
> hurtling down the sidewalk,
> O small son of mine.

*

NEAR THE END of our stay we drove west, north, inland, then to the Atlantic coast. We could never resist beaches, even if only Malcolm took full advantage of them. When tumultuous waves hurled themselves onshore, Malcolm launched a makeshift javelin at them.

In Lisbon we sat in a café, listening to some U.S. sailors obliviously chatting in full voice about the locals. Belatedly we noticed Malcolm's absence. A moment ago he'd been with me. I rushed out to the busy street. This kind of thing often happened. I would be walking somewhere crowded with him and he would disappear. In a panic I would look around and find him lagging in some un-suspected corner my eye had not reached. He had a knack for such vanishings.

Around the Lisbon street corner there he stood, looking bemused.

We contracted with a babysitting agency that guaranteed our healthy white child would not be sold to the highest bidder. A well-brought-up young woman tended him while we went to a fado club and I got food poisoning. A snapshot lingered from our stay in Portugal. On a golden beach our golden Malcolm is dashing across the golden sand.

*

WHEN WE GOT back to Nova Scotia, Alison continued to adapt well to her new, and my old, church and community. I was mis-erable, as if to fulfill the adage that you can't go home anymore. What made me more depressed was that our best friends were about to depart. John, a manager at the nearby agricultural co-op, was taking up a two-year post in St. Lucia, where he was going to get a feed mill built. He and Celia had two sons of their own, elder-statesmen playmates for Malcolm. Once one of them had inadver-tently plugged Malcolm in the centre of the forehead with a lawn dart. "Mom," Malcolm had asked afterward, "how bad can you get hurt when a big kid shows you how to have fun?"

With our remaining money, we went to St. Lucia, greeted at the airport by our friends and the overwhelming heat. One day John was driving Malcolm and me somewhere when he stopped to pick up a hitchhiker. Malcolm tactlessly asked the man why he was so black. "Because of the sun," he said.

One scorching day we went to the beach. The blue Caribbean glittered as I wandered off and lay down, dazed by the heat. Alison and Malcolm, a life ring encircling him, ran into the water. I saw a flurry in the distance. Hurrying back, I learned that a crashing wave had wrenched Malcolm's hand from Alison's. He might have been swept to the Bahamas had he not clung to the ring. For years to come a cold shudder gripped me when I remembered how we had almost lost him.

*

WHEN WE RETURNED home Granny tried to entertain Malcolm by writing tales of the cats and dogs who'd been her beloved pets in childhood. At some point, however, the stories went wrong and the animals come to a sad end as if her loyalty was to the truth, not the crafting of a happy-ever-after ending. She gave up, possibly realizing she had written a deeply depressing document.

One summer day I happened to be standing on the lawn in front of the house. Something made me look up. Malcolm was straddling the roof's tall apex. He must have got out through an upstairs window and climbed higher. He sat there far above, looking calm and contemplative, almost smug.

"What the hell are you doing?" I yelled. I urged him down the steep, asphalt-shingled slant, but not to do it too quickly.

He called down, "Don't tell Granny! Don't tell Mummy!" Perhaps I should have been pleased he confided in me. Maybe the trouble was that he didn't fear a scolding, but did fear his secret prowess would be revealed.

In one of their games, Malcolm would say to his mother, "Be Travis, Mama!" Alison batted around a foam rubber disc, spun it at him, and he hit it with his "sword," which was also a magic wand — you pointed it at bad guys, and they turned into good guys.

*

MALCOLM HAD AN inner life we could only guess at and certainly couldn't access. After he learned to print he invented a character called "Malcolm McTosh," who seemed to be an alter ego, a doppel-gänger if not exactly an imaginary pal.

> Dear dada, 1 day Malcolm MacTosh was eating a hog-amogaplant when all of a sudden a streak of eye ball laser almost hit him. Then he saw Slime Stick. And Malcolm MacTosh had to yell, 'SHOO A WAY! SHOO A WAY!' Then Malcolm MacTosh kicked Slime Stick, Out. Then Malcolm MacTosh walked into the house, taking his magic argon with him, and ate his dinner (fried hogamogaplant sandwiches).

Evidently Malcolm MacTosh was also a superhero of sorts. I was a little uncertain where exactly Malcolm McTosh lived, other than in Malcolm's head:

As he related the story,

> One day Malcolm MacIntosh decided to go to earth. He saw all the pollution. He brought his giant sling-shot to earth. He started shooting garbage cans into outer space, but a comet came and smashed them and garbage flew all over outer space. Malcolm MacIntosh gave up that idea. He decided to take his super-duper compost machine from his planet. He decided to test it. He Put a garbage can in it and turned it on. Then he aimed it at the ground. He fired it and a tree appeared. The nice thing about it is, that it runs on garbage. Soon the mayor of New York city came and

complained to Malcolm MacIntosh. He said that it was letting out tons of smoke. He said that the people couldn't see their own hands. To be continued....

*

MY BROTHER BILL, a long-time Haligonian, lived within easy driving distance. To me Malcolm had always seemed a dour baby and toddler, rather as if he disapproved of his parents and regretted that he couldn't have done better. This was not the case with his sole paternal uncle. From the first moment he saw Bill, his face lit up like a flashlight snapping on. With joyous mutual recognition they grinned at each other. On weekends Bill sometimes drove the hundred miles from his one-bedroom bachelor apartment to see us. Malcolm eagerly awaited these visits. To Malcolm he was, as Alison termed it, "a mythic millenium figure."

With Malcolm he devilishly played a game that was designed to gross out Mom. He'd always been on uneasy terms with her. Knowing that she was averse to anything suggesting eros, he introduced Malcolm to a practice that was in fact not a little creepy. He and Malcolm indulged in mutual chin-sucking. It drove Mom into a frenzy. "Stop, stop!" she'd say, moaning and rushing out of the room.

Bill seated him at the table ten minutes before supper and taught him to clink spoon and fork, calling "COOK BRING FOOD!" and "COOK BRING WINE!" and "COOK BRING WOMEN!" Actually the only potential cook in sight would have been Bill's current girlfriend, a tall, dark power-company executive named Deb, who sometimes accompanied him.

Bill would sometimes lie down for a snooze on the living room sofa, sleeping at one end, Malcolm at the other. Some minutes later he would come awake, especially on festive occasions like Christmas, suddenly aware he was half-smothered with balloons and other debris Malcolm had gathered and carefully layered on top of him. "If you need anything else, Uncle Billy," he would say, "just let me know."

Bill had a repertoire of pranks for Malcolm's entertainment, like pretending to salt one of his toes prior to its being devoured. He taught Malcolm a favourite song, "We're Off to See the Wild West Show." I didn't know what show Bill may have meant.

As for Malcolm and I, we had mutually satisfying sadomasochistic games. I would hoist him on my shoulders and gravely warn him that he was astride an "unruly camel." I'd shake and quake, while Malcolm hung on desperately, shrieking in mixed pleasure and terror. As another enjoyable torment, I'd stand on a chair near him like a leopard lingering watchfully on an overhead branch. I'd say in hushed tones, "Unbeknownst to the little animal ..." Malcolm would scurry away from the predator about to pounce on him. Mom disapproved. "He's going to hate you when he grows up," she said.

For the time being he didn't hate me, though. When winter came, Malcolm was especially intrigued by "tree popsicles," the sun blazing through the sheaths of ice hanging from trees. Malcolm used the icicles, some as long as himself, as swords or magic wands. You pointed them at "bad guys" and said "Bye bye Zammie," and they turned into good guys.

While Alison tried to set an example of healthy outdoor exercise by skiing up and down hills, he'd spend an hour eating ice off things. When chastised for speaking impolitely to her, he said, "I know I'm being nasty to you, Mama, but I can't help it." She worked on his tone of voice when he addressed grown-ups. He had no notion of the need for respect, and obviously regarded them as equals. She found it was difficult to convince him he should be polite, when Mom and I spoke as a matter of course in tones of appalling discourtesy.

However, he was opposed to nastiness. When a kid came around to do coasting on our hill and started to push Malcolm around he backed off and said, "Wait a minute, Matthew. Let's not be nasty. Let's be nice and have fun."

*

IN HIS ROOM Malcolm housed a petting zoo or captive menagerie of bears, monkeys, and assorted dolls ruled over by a small fuzzy scarlet stuffed creature he christened Peter Pig. Adapting "Robin Hood, Robin Hood, Riding Through the Glen," the theme song of the fifties TV hit *The Adventures of Robin Hood*, Bill would croon, "Peter Pig, Peter Pig, Riding Through the Glen." But he stumbled over the next line, "With his band of men" because a pig leading a group of men didn't sound right. He lamely settled on "With his band of ... other pigs."

The only time we managed to separate Peter Pig and Malcolm was when we went to Chapel Hill, North Carolina, in midwinter to see my friend Elizabeth, a Mississippi novelist and short-story writer perhaps best known for the novella *The Light in the Piazza* and who might have struck the imperceptive as the archetypal Southern Belle. I had met her in the early 1970s when we both lived in Montreal. Alison and I assured Malcolm that Peter Pig would be perfectly fine for a week in the parking lot of Halifax International Airport.

Our trip began cheerfully; when aboard the flight a good-humoured Delta flight attendant had Malcolm make a goodwill announcement over the P.A. system. Landed at Raleigh-Durham, we rented a car. We stayed briefly in Chapel Hill, then ferry-toured the Outer Banks and drove as far south as Charleston, eating truly fresh shrimp and avoiding fried chitlins. As a childless mature couple, Elizabeth, a thoroughgoing Mississippian, and her stolid, granite-jawed husband John, a Britisher, were unused to having someone of Malcolm's age around, and Malcolm was unused to being around people like them. No matter: he became instant friends with their next-door neighbour's kid.

＊

UNCLE BILL SOMETIMES neatly penned a mock itinerary for him during his visits. For the Lobster Carnival that summer his pompous detail befitted a royal tour:

6:30 a.m.	Wake up and proceed downstairs
6:30–7:15	Watch favourite TV Prog.
7:15–8:00	Get dressed
8:00–8:30	Breakfast
8:30–8:45	Proceed to hairdresser's
8:45–9:15	Haircut (Possibly Spiked)
9:15–9:30	Depart hairdresser's, travel to Pictou
9:30–10:15	Arrive Pictou, walk about Pictou, visit Naylor's and Tim Horton's
10:15–10:30	Depart Tim Horton's and Proceed to Dock
10:30	Board boat
10:30–11:15	Cruise harbour
11:15–12:00	Depart dock and proceed to explore Carnival displays
12:00–12:45	Lobster lunch provided by Uncle Bill
12:45–1:30	Walk about, observe Carnival activities (if any)
1:30	Depart Pictou (We're out of Here!)
1:30–2:00	Travel Caribou Island
2:00	Arrive Caribou Island

2:00–3:30	Examine beach, drink Pepsi, Watch for Girls, Get snacks at Canteen (Perhaps even go in the water)
3:30	Depart Caribou Island and Proceed to Granny's
4:00	Arrive Granny's and Relate Day's Activities
4:15	Open

EQUIPPED WITH A *Star Trek* lunchbox and a Harvard sweater, Malcolm would catch a bus for school at the edge of Scotsburn, a couple of miles away. He was more or less content with his teachers, who seemed to me a gentle bunch. As an outsider, he got bullying from a few schoolmates but on a minor scale. Like him, his schoolmates were mostly descendants of the Scots who were forced from their Highland crofts in the late eighteenth and early nineteenth centuries and crossed the North Atlantic to interbreed and set down roots in this unpromising place. But no doubt it was better than starving in the Highlands.

Malcolm made his theatrical debut in Bethel Presbyterian Church's Christmas pageant and Scotsburn Elementary School's Christmas concert. The "Friendly Beasts" part of the program included his solo:

> *I, said the cow, all white and red*
> *I gave him my manger for a bed*
> *I gave him my hay to pillow his head*
> *I, said the cow, all white and red*

*

AMONG THE GOOD friends he made was Holly, a very blond girl his own age, who lived on the farm back of the highway below us. Her father piped Mozart into his barn; it was said to aid the milk production of those friendly beasts, the Holsteins, who were black and white, not red and white, not the creamy brown of the Jerseys Dad had raised. Her parents made a home movie starring Holly and Malcolm. At their age, a premature adult, I would have been embarrassed to see it screened. But they sat on the couch enraptured, a pair of singletons absorbed by their performances.

His interests were gastronomic, not athletic. For his birthday he vetoed a quiet dinner party: he wanted a "proper" party. When Alison offered to make a mocha torte, her specialty, he said, "I don't want to hurt your feelings, Mama, but I would like a *proper* cake, chocolate. With roses and 'Happy Birthday, Malcolm' on it. In the shape of a snowman." Alison said she didn't know how to make such a cake. I got someone else to make it.

As a contribution to the party games, he cut out the tails for pin-the-tail-on-the-donkey game, and said, "Now, Mama, we want to do as much as possible the day *before* the party." On the special day Alison and I were awakened by Malcolm at our beside, saying, "Now Mama and Dada, I want today to be a *very special* day. I don't want anything to go wrong ..." As he left for school, he said, "When the guests come in, I want to be able to press a button and down from the ceiling will come spaghetti and balloons." This was not arranged. When Alison was about to drive off to pick up the guests, Malcolm wearily gave her the news, "I'm afraid there are going to be a few more people coming than we planned, Mama." There were.

*

WHEN SUMMER CAME Bill and I took Malcolm to a farmers' market. When he swung himself on a guardrail, a lady at a table said,

"Don't fall and hurt yourself." Malcolm replied, "It's all right. I'm a trained professional."

*

ONE MUGGY JULY day I drove Mom from small town to town, looking for a couch she could add to the bedsitter suite she'd carved out to give herself more privacy. That evening a TV program about cardiopulmonary resuscitation was on. Pushing down on the person having cardiac arrest, breathing into the person's mouth. Mom asked thoughtfully if I knew how to do CPR. I didn't.

In the small hours that night the wind picked up and rain began to pelt. Mom, always a restive sleeper, began to rush about the house, slamming windows shut.

Something went badly wrong. Her heart, her badly hurting heart. Hoping it was a false alarm, I muttered, "I don't think this is real." Her moans rose as I drove fast the five miles to the small-town hospital in Pictou, the relocated replacement of the hospital in which my mother had given birth to me and my brothers. A doctor was roused at his home. Before he got to her side, Mom was dead. She had died on Bill's birthday.

When Malcolm got up that morning, we gently told him what had happened. I wasn't sure he was taking it in. I had trouble taking it in myself. I was at least able to compose an obituary to go in a newspaper.

SUTHERLAND, MARY ISABEL
Suddenly at Sutherland-Harris Memorial Hospital, Pictou, Nova Scotia, early on Saturday July 27, the wife of the later Russell Sutherland. Born in 1910 to Alexander and Isabel (Fraser) MacHardy of McClellan's Mountain, Mary Sutherland was a graduate of Pictou

Academy and the Nova Scotia Teachers' College, and taught at country schools in Pictou County. A farm wife in Heathbell and Hardwood Hill, she gallantly and devotedly cared for her handicapped son Hughie, who predeceased her. She was an active member of Bethel Presbyterian Church, Scotsburn, and a former president and secretary of the Burning Bush chapter of the Atlantic Missionary Society. As well, she was a volunteer quilter for the Canadian Red Cross, and supported Bethel Presbyterian Ladies' Aid and the Izaak Walton Killam Hospital for Children. She loved unstintingly her family, home, and church, and cherished her good neighbours. An enthusiastic hobbyist and gardener, she had a lively curiosity about people and events. Vigorous and self-reliant to the end, she will be remembered for her warmth, wit, and loving kindness by all who knew her, and by her sons Bill and Fraser, her daughter-in-law Alison, and her grandson Malcolm. Donations in her memory may be made to the Atlantic Cerebral Palsy Association, 90 Mount Edward Rd., Charlottetown, P.E.I. CIA 5S6.

After the funeral, at the edge of the open grave, Malcolm stared down into the deep hole where Granny lay in her casket. I was afraid he might topple in.

Later he began to weep because he hadn't got a chance to say goodbye to her.

Bill, who inherited half the farm, likely would have allowed us to live there in perpetuity if we wanted to. Malcolm was doing well in school, if the *W*s ("Works to Potential") on his report cards were any indication. No problem about reading skills. "He has progressed far beyond grade level expectations in this area."

If I'd filled out a report card on my own progress I would have been less positive. No sooner had I arrived in Pictou County than I wanted out. It was hard to isolate why. The people around me were just ordinary people: good, bad, or indifferent. I felt under house arrest. I had developed an all-consuming hatred of the noisy, dangerous, and destructive all-terrain vehicles (spring, summer, fall) and snowmobiles (winter) roaring along the abandoned railway bed that crossed our lane. To some, their operators were ignorable or tolerated pests. To me they were besiegers. They summed up my discontents. I told myself that it was much quieter here than in the city. The chug of a tractor on a field, even the intermittent accelerated whine of a chainsaw — these assaults on the senses were nothing to what a city brought. Even on a residential street, the leafblower, the snowblower, the jackhammer, the electric or motorized lawnmower, the jabber and shriek of a family party in someone's back garden, the surf or stutter of traffic, the random wail of a siren — all these were sounds of a city. Why, then, was noise in the countryside so disturbing? Because it didn't belong there, didn't conform to my idea of what the countryside should be like.

I feared Malcolm in the long term might turn into some insular, parochial, rural lout. I had been brought up here. Did that mean I was a lout? I tried to convince myself that, at least partly, we should move for his sake. If nothing else, to give him a more sophisticated milieu. Though leaving this place was imperative to me, it was sad Malcolm had to leave the friends he had made. He'd be leaving behind the Beavers, those junior Boy Scouts. His Scotsburn school report cards had been uniformly good, or at least no more or less anodyne than the ones given to every parent.

> Malcolm is a favourite author in our class, as he continues to chronicle the ongoing saga of "Malcolm McTosh — MM." He has certainly progressed as a

writer. He is a very confident and competent speaker.
He has a rich receptive and active vocabulary which
makes him an able listener, speaker, reader and writer.

In Toronto, the city that was our obvious destination, he would
not be able to climb the row of Russet apple trees below the house,
scaling the heights. He would miss our late March–early April rituals of spring: an expedition to a deep-woods sugar shack for pancakes, baked beans, and maple syrup; miss the green curlicues of
fiddleheads surfacing in the marsh we owned below the highway.
Miss socializing with an atypical Mi'kmaq family — Michael, a
housing inspector, had an M.A. in European history from Harvard.
Malcolm would never have another chance to see a begloved
Princess Anne make an escorted call at Scotsburn's principal in-
dustry, Scotsburn Dairy.

*

FROM TIME TO time, and from far away, I'd get long letters from my
friend Edward, the world traveller, poet and translator, intermittent
teacher of English as a foreign or second language to Mexicans,
Brazilians, and Indonesians. Due to his misadventures he likely
held the world record for smashed eyeglasses and lost passports.
He'd touched down in most of the countries on five continents,
starting while he was in graduate school in Texas, after he'd been
apprehended at the Mexican border and got a suspended sentence
for pot possession and fled to Mexico. A heroic hedonist, an alcoholic homosexual with a prodigious talent for trouble, his penchant for young hustlers often inflicted damage. He was moral
yet amoral, super-rational yet serially impulsive, hypochondriac
yet tough, arrogant yet diffident, solipsistic yet insanely generous.
A superb translator — he read, spoke, and wrote four languages

fluently — he was a pioneer of explicitly gay poetry, not just in Canada, anywhere. Despising authority, he was an exile who yearned for yet rejected intimacy. Pedantically aloof, gravely polite, he could make friends from every culture, race, or underclass. Among his friends, he inspired fondness and clucking disapproval. He hated his own country so corrosively it practically amounted to love. I once sent him a snapshot of Malcolm smelling a flower, which he told his fellow teachers friends was a childhood portrait of himself.

One day I got a phone call from the Department of External Affairs in Ottawa, telling me Edward had been run over while lying on a Bangkok street. The official was dunning me, along with his other friends, to help pay for his hospital expenses. After consulting with Alison, I replied I could send a one-time sum. Or the diplomats could ship him to Canada, and I'd accept delivery. Cutting its losses, External Affairs chose the latter. At the Halifax airport, I picked him up. Edward sat in a wheelchair, grizzled and ashen, hands folded atop a giant vinyl suitcase straddling the armrests, one leg in a cast, a granny shawl over his shoulders.

When we got home, there came a volley of barks: our burglar-alarm poodle, Darcy, successor to Holly, doing his duty. The barking roused Alison, who groggily appeared in a nightdress. She escorted Edward to what had been my mother's self-designed combination kitchen and sitting room.

Sequestered, he rejected radio, television, and our pets. "Anyone who would give house room to a dog," he declared, "would give house room to a mongoloid idiot," thus managing to insult both our poodle and Alison's mentally handicapped brother. Quaking like some harshly punitive parent, he scolded Malcolm on his unsuitable choice of friends, a wrathful stabbing finger invoking divine wrath. Though indignant at these reproaches from a stranger, Malcolm considered our guest as blustery weather that had blown in and would soon blow out. He was right. Our brain-damaged guest subsided to one rage a week.

Meanwhile, I was trying to figure out where he could go next. He had to go somewhere. In the next few months we had to sell our home, pack and ship several tons of belongings, find a place to live in Toronto, and get ourselves and our pets there. Peterborough, Ontario, wasn't far from his hometown of Lindsay with its resident cousins, only two hours' drive from Toronto. Alison got paperwork in motion with social agencies while I lobbied his cousins, whose names I'd extracted from shreds of correspondence. One of them agreed to pick up him at a bus terminal on his arrival and take him to stopgap lodgings.

It was early May. A committed records keeper, Alison supplied him with a thick binder of key documents, including a typed chronology of his comeback, compiled to make up for his memory loss. He'd mellowed toward the poodle, describing him as "a European heiress down on her luck." His wounds had healed, on the surface at least; he was mobile; he was *compos mentis* enough to ably edit a sermon Alison was to deliver at a Bethel church. I flew with him to Toronto and packed him into a minivan booked for Peterborough, not far away.

We sold or gave away everything we didn't want, and shipped the rest. Alison boarded a plane with the two cats, Becky and Sally, in a Sky Kennel, and Darcy the poodle. Malcolm, and I set off overland by car. We crossed the Maine border and navigated curves, hills, and gravel pits on the way to Bangor. At Newport we found a bed-and-breakfast. A grating, grinding brake drum halted us.

Equipped with a new brake pad, we wound our way through hilly Vermont and upstate New York, where we stayed with an expatriate writer friend in Saratoga Springs. Malcolm was a patient, uncomplaining companion. This was what it was to be a child: to just go along for the ride. The dreariness of long-distance driving did get to him eventually. After we crossed into Ontario on the Thousand Islands bridge near Gananoque and got on the serially monotonous 401 highway, he resorted to never-ending reiterations of a maddening, nonsensical ditty.

A nervous driver at best, I wasn't looking forward to twelve lanes of traffic. My fears were reinforced on entering metropolitan Toronto. I kept looking for a slow lane, but there wasn't one. I headed for what turned out to be a premature exit, and stayed idling half in, half out, waiting for a chance to get back in the stream, whimpering to myself. I overshot an expressway, though its lanes were closed by barrels anyway. I missed another possible exit but got the next one. Ordinary streets were a balm. I pulled into what was to be our new street. Past the rear of a public-housing apartment building, I turned down a lane and parked in a gap behind our back fence.

*

ALISON HAD WANTED a south-facing backyard. On a scouting trip earlier I found one and the house that went with it. It was only a few houses away from busy Bathurst Street and Hillcrest Community School, which Malcolm would attend. Next door was an animal hospital, bound to be useful.

If ever a house fitted the definition of a teardown our new house was it. Not that we were about to move out. Our landlord was obliging about effecting repairs but employed a comprehensively incompetent handyman to do them. Malcolm's room was a door away from Alison's and mine, in the other direction two doors away from my office.

At Hillcrest he soon made friends with a gentle giant of a half-Russian boy named Nathan who lived with his father in a heroically cluttered house down the hill, and with Adrian, a curly-haired, half-Italian boy whose father would drop him off with us. Adrian's parents had jobs, so it was convenient to park him with us for an hour at the start of a school day. He and Malcolm and Adrian would happily deal each other role-playing Magic cards — impersonating wizards, it would seem. They babbled away in their sorcery-prone, self-constructed world; I couldn't tell who was ahead. Then they left for school, trooping past a crossing guard who needlessly held up a STOP sign at the red light.

Likely at Alison's prompting, he sent progress reports to his godparents. He could swim and bike. He reported that with new friends he built forts in the alley and fashioned a bow and arrow, a slingshot, and a trident, and a spear out of a very sharp lamb bone. He played computer games non-stop and, incited by Alison, read Gerald Durrell's anima-seeking books and C.S. Lewis's Narnia books. It wasn't her influence that attracted him to ghosts, poltergeists, vampires, and ouija boards.

*

ONE WINTER DAY I looked through the glass pane of the back door. Malcolm was coming home from school to have lunch. He came through the back gate and then halted in the middle of the yard, unmoving in the snow, every nerve at the alert, intensely listening. What he was hearing I didn't know and couldn't guess.

At Hillcrest Community School he earned a certificate stating that he had qualified as a conflict manager (at Scotsburn he had received a "Happy Helper Award" for "taking classroom responsibilities so seriously.") I wondered what conflicts he had to manage. He graduated from a horsemanship riding camp. T'was all to the good. I wanted him to try as many (drug-free) activities as possible in the hope one would stick.

*

MY BRAIN-DAMAGED FRIEND had not been thriving. Edward was shuttled from place to place in Peterborough, but was discontented and unmanageable everywhere. After much bureaucratic liaising, Alison got him into a rehabilitation program at a downtown Toronto hospital. While there, an infection developed where a metal plate had been implanted in Bangkok. On July 1, Canada Day, surgeons successfully cut out the infected bone and did a graft. When Malcolm paused from performing calisthenics with pieces of medical furniture on our visits, Edward, always the teacher, instructed Malcolm on points of grammar. Once we took Edward outside the hospital for some fresh air. Malcolm occupied himself by chasing pigeons. Edward remarked, "He is aggrandizing his territory."

*

THE DAY I received my prostate cancer diagnosis I spent the afternoon fitfully reading a grim offprint from the *Scientific American* about prostate cancer that the specialist had given me in lieu of a full explanation. That evening Alison and I watched Malcolm take part in a dance performance his class was putting on. "He can't dance a step," his teacher had said, "but he makes up for it in enthusiasm." Indeed he did. But I wasn't taking it in. Everything had become painfully hallucinogenic.

I took him to a coffee shop to tell him that I was going to have surgery. Something caught in my throat when I tried to tell him there was a remote possibility I could die during the operation. Just as difficult, I tried to tell him how much he meant to me. Uncomfortable, his discomfort mirroring mine, he said, "I know you love me, Dad."

He wrote his cousins Becca and Joe about me:

Mum was talking to your mum the other evening and she told me that you were very worried about how I was feeling now that I know that my Dad has cancer.

I appreciate your concern, but really it seems silly to get upset and worried. They told me that only one person in three hundred dies of it. It's not as if it was a very life-threatening disease, even though he might be going to have an operation and feel sick for a while.

It sometimes seems as if too much fuss is being made of it all, especially when Mum hovers over Dad a lot. Sickening, when she could be hovering over ME.

Dad sometimes seems grumpy and too often "Not in the mood," but I don't pay any attention to this and go right ahead and bug him. And I make sure he doesn't get away with anything like changing the channel on the TV without asking my permission.

I made them promise to be sure and tell me if anything goes wrong, so I don't need to worry if something's going on that I don't know.

So, let's worry about it if it happens, and not get too fussed about it now.

Thank you for thinking about me, but don't worry.

*

THE STREETCAR BUMPED and lurched the three of us toward Lake Ontario. We had a duty to perform. In my lap was a bag. In the bag was a box. In the box was another bag, holding the remains of my friend. Almost reaching the age of fifty-eight, he had died from a heart attack in a welfare rooming house a month earlier. The box had lain, a brown rectangular reproach, atop a filing cabinet in my basement. His will, which he'd copied from legal boilerplate six years earlier, was clear. He did not want his body to be returned to, interred in, or otherwise retained in his birthplace, the town of Lindsay, Ontario, an hour and a half's drive northeast. His body was offered to medical science. If it were deemed unacceptable, it was to be cremated, the ashes scattered on the nearest river, lake, or sea. The Don River was perhaps closer to my home, but I didn't want to deposit the last of an old friend in a toxic trench. Better the wide expanse of Lake Ontario, the Iroquoian lake of shining waters.

The rear doors parted where the lakeshore skirted a hurtling boulevard. We looked for an inconspicuous spot, but people thronged the strip of parkland this cloudless Sunday afternoon of high summer. A few dogs competed in the hundred-metre dash. Canada geese stomped across our path, mugging bread crusts from picnickers who organized cook-outs and spread blankets by the boles of maples and elms. A heat-haze lay on the lake, obscuring the farther shore. Alison was cheerful and reverent. Malcolm was unreadable. Maybe he thought that what I was about to do I did to all my friends, once I had finished with them.

Since the next act would violate several municipal bylaws, I nervously glanced around. Atop a knoll loomed a knot of tall Africans, curious about our burial customs. To hell with it. I gingerly disgorged the bag of gritty sand into the murk, afraid the backwash would cling to my legs. Edward's friend and publisher in San Francisco had asked that a few ashes be sent to him for use in a Buddhist ceremony. I wasn't up to it. I carefully shook out the bag, the water clouding.

*

A NEIGHBOUR DOWN the street knocked on the door one evening. He had caught Malcolm and his gentle-giant friend prying off a decal from his car parked in the back lane. A collecting mania for

auto-dealer decals had developed among the preteens. We made
him apologize. In the spirit of forgiveness the neighbour took him
off to McDonald's for a treat.

At home entertainment became a routine. We played backgammon and Monopoly and watched *Star Trek*. He became addicted to
The Simpsons, I supposed because it was so subversive. Becky and
Sally were pleased his door was open again; he'd kept it closed to
thwart invasions of other pets. Timothy, his guinea pig, had died
of an apparent heart attack. As we did with other deceased pets we
buried him in the backyard. Once he got his own place, Malcolm
said, he would get a Vietnamese potbellied pig. The only trouble
about the cats, he complained, was that they each took about half
an hour to settle down at night, which kept him awake. He wrote
Uncle Bill, "I hope you don't have the same problem with Deb, not
that it's any of my business."

Mocking his own diary-writing style he added,

> My cousins arrived from B.C. Their plane crash-
> landed in our backyard. We managed to get them out
> and more important their presents without bursting
> into flame. Then we decorated the tree.

A few days later, he wrote, he read to Nell, his youngest cousin,
a book about a woman slowly losing her mind.

> But she didn't seem to like it. How strange.

*

WE ENTRAINED FOR Windsor, Ontario. Bill was there, commuting
across the border to attend law school in Detroit. He had showed
a flash of the old devilishly teasing uncle when he stalled about

taking Malcolm for a promised swim in his highrise's swimming pool. Furious, Malcolm hurled a pair of goggles at him. Because I got a brief gig as a writer-in-library in frigid Winnipeg, Malcolm had a single-parent family for a couple of months. He and Alison were able to enjoy Malcolm's piebald pet mouse Richard without my objecting to its scooting across the kitchen table to sample the butter. Richard later became a casualty of the cats.

*

BILL MOVED ON to Florida; he was setting up a law practice and we were going to see him again. Prior to our visit he composed his usual itemized numbered agenda for his "MSPN (Medium Sized Perfect Nephew)":

1. Hunt Alligators
2. Chase Alligators In Everglades On Airboat
3. Watch Girls
4. Swim And Watch Girls
5. Find Mickey Mouse At Disney World
6. Search For Manatee In Canals
7. Lay In Sun (On Beach), Read Stories, Get a Tan, Watch Girls
8. Eat Lots Of Shrimp
9. Go Rollerblading On A Smooth Safe Place And Show Off For Girls

An ideal agenda for Bill, if not necessarily for Malcolm. When we got in Bill took us to his self-catering apartment in Pompano Beach. He took his tour-guide duties seriously, taking us to scenic sedate Coral Gables, where one of Bill's law friends resided, to affluent palm-dotted Boca Raton, to walkable bayside Coconut Grove, and to the stucco glories of the Miami Beach art-deco strip. In between we cruised and crawled through miscellaneous anonymous shopping malls and plazas and made eight swim stops for Malcolm.

The next day we made the two-hundred-mile drive to Orlando and the precincts of Disney World, tailor-made for Bill and Malcolm, though not for me. In Seminole territory we took an airboat ride through the Everglades and snacked on alligator nuggets, which did indeed taste like chicken.

When, back in Pompano Beach, Bill's girlfriend, Deb, arrived we headed for a Thai restaurant in a strip mall. At our table Malcolm slumped asleep, Deb seized him and pranced out to make him sleep on the back seat of Bill's car, locking him in. I wasn't in favour of confining my small son to a locked car in a mall parking lot, however that might suit his elders' convenience. After brooding a moment I snarled, "Next time ask me first." I brought Malcolm inside.

That summer Alison, Malcolm, and I paid a brief return visit to Pictou County. As given to melodramatic gestures as Alison, at Mom's grave Malcolm fell to his knees, his forehead resting against her tombstone.

In September he no longer trooped down a back lane and across street to school. For two years he would attend a middle school of mildly alternative tendencies. Students were supposed to undertake contracts to complete projects. He completed his projects but took little interest in sports. Maybe that was natural. My interest in them, once intense, was now minimal, and Alison's aversion to sports was such that she would start yelling at me if she caught me watching football on TV. At Delta, sports weren't emphasized. In any case Malcolm wasn't the kind of kid who would be picked for a team. So far, the extent of my encouraging athletics was to occasionally throw a ball back and forth. I used to take him down to a community rink on winter days, though I couldn't skate and he didn't want to take lessons. At least he had learned to ski and swim in Pictou.

Unlike his coevals, the tweens and teens who clogged street-cars and buses with backpacks apparently filled with construction-site rubble, Malcolm only had to bike two short streets west, then plunge down the hill to his new school. I tried not to think about the traffic. Maybe I should have, because Alison discovered Sally, one of our Nova Scotia cats, dead in the lane, apparently hit by a car.

At Delta Malcolm seemed to specialize in losing things. I wrote his teacher that among Malcolm's missing school materials were a literature notebook, a composition and grammar booklet, a problem-solving math textbook, a science assignment, and three out of four of his marked literature papers that should have come back after his second contract period.

After a thorough search, I wrote, these items were unlocatable. They were not in Malcolm's schoolbag, nor had they been with him when he visited friends. They were not in his locker or in his desk.

This led us to one or more of three conclusions. Either they were mislaid somewhere around the school, they were stolen, or they were picked up by someone else accidentally.

I wrote,

> Malcolm will have another look around the school before handing this note to you. If some or all materials are still missing after he's done so, we would like you to enquire whether anyone, students or staff, may have found them. Malcolm is very upset about the loss and he accepts his responsibility for it. However, it is possible that the loss was at least partly outside his control. We will of course pay to have the materials replaced but we would like to know what actually happened so that we can ensure it will not happen again.

It did happen again.

*

WHEN MALCOLM AND I flew to Halifax in July the only thing with four wheels available to rent at the airport was a Brobdingnagian SUV whose cab was so high I practically needed a stepladder to get into it. However, it got us to Moncton — I peered over the steering wheel all the way — where we ate barbecued salmon with John and Celia. John was now an executive with Co-op Atlantic. We made stops to see Bill in Halifax and drove around to friends and acquaintances scattered in the wooded hills, small towns, and back roads of Pictou County, shacking up with them for the night when necessary. One of them, Ian, had a vendetta against raccoons and impressed and dismayed us by dashing to his shotgun and blasting away at them. After a farewell supper with Bill in his apartment we got the SUV to the car-rental outlet in one large piece.

*

BACK IN TORONTO Malcolm entered the next most desirable thing to a private school — which had been Alison's experience and would have been her preference — the demanding International Baccalaureate program inserted into a nearby high school, Vaughan Road Collegiate, this one a stiff pedal uphill. Based in Geneva, Switzerland, the I.B. gave accreditation organized around an inter-disciplinary core curriculum. That was the theory, anyway.

Alison, not I, made him do his homework. We tapped a neigh-bour around the corner, a translator, to supplement his French, but language learning wasn't his priority. In Vaughan Road's lar-ger student body he was immersed in Toronto's vaunted multicul-turalism. Small aggregations of Black people were ranged against Filipino cabals, and his classmates had names like Verschaging, Vu-Fushad, and Aftzal. Within the I.B. program were Russian and

Indian students, and Malcolm would regale me with reports of their academic prowess and impersonate their charming accents. It was a clean, well-run school. One day, supporting some cause, the kids demonstrated out front, urging drivers to honk their horns in solidarity. A Russian girl charmingly called out, "Conk your corn! Conk your corn!"

*

WE'D HAD A scare. Alison's period was late. Aged forty-eight, she took a pregnancy test. We discussed the possibility of an abortion and I told her it was her body, her decision. In the non-event she wasn't pregnant.

Though Malcolm had no brothers and sisters, he did have cousins roughly the same age. When he saw Martin, son of Alison's sister Polly, at his home or ours, food often figured, perhaps fittingly because Martin's German father was a trained pastry chef who operated a gourmet shop. Malcolm would devour the unsold fruit flans brought home from the shop, remarking that it was rewarding to have an uncle who was a pastry chef. I contributed to his education by taking the boys to eat jerk chicken with rice and peas (actually kidney beans); sushi here and there; dim sum in Chinatown; in Little India tandoori chicken, salty or sweet milkshake-like lassi, and paan, a mouthful of seeds wrapped in a betel leaf. Once, while eating out, Martin told him the Chinese pancakes they ordered were towelettes. To his delight Malcolm wiped his face with one. They cooked together as well, whether at Martin's house, where they would play with the spices, or at mine, where they tried to outdo each other in the number of toppings on their sandwiches. An inveterate fridge raider, Malcolm introduced his cousin to pungent Thai shrimp paste and used ghee, clarified butter, in Kraft Dinner. What he didn't finish at night he stockpiled in the fridge as a resource for next morning's breakfast. I was proud of his prowess as a junior gourmand.

Malcolm and he managed to get into trouble: the first time Martin came over to our house they managed to break half of the slats in the futon by jumping on it. They explored stink bombs, one of which had poodle hair that smelled much like an electrical fire and brought me down from my office in a hurry.

They would lie in sleeping bags and Malcolm would tell Martin movie plots. Martin introduced Malcolm to his slingshot, and to the bow and arrows he inherited from their Uncle Rob. They spent a lot of time hunting squirrels, never successfully. Then came firecrackers. No one had any objections to this at first, even when Malcolm threw one into a fireplace, until they began blowing up jam jars in the alley, enraging several neighbours, including a man whose wife had recently been mugged. For his eleventh birthday Martin was given a chemistry set; he and Malcolm added aftershave, and set it to cook.

Once they went with Alison to Ontario Place, a theme park and entertainment playground, and got kicked off the bumper boats for running into the corner for the whole ride. Malcolm always had a wicked, mischievous streak, an impishness and joy in making mischief. His eyes sparkled when he discovered Minna, Martin's Labrador, reacted enthusiastically to "Hello?" *every single time.* His practical jokes included putting a car freshener in the hood of Alison's parka.

One Thanksgiving we journeyed out to Polly's place near the village of Erin, taking in the county fair. I was cajoled into boarding a ride called the Octopus. It didn't look so bad from the ground. Little did I know the horrors that the ride held. To Malcolm's delight I almost lost the french fries I had just eaten. For cousin Nell Vandermeer, six years younger, one of the many amazing things about Malcolm was his talent for make-believe. When she was three Malcolm and their cousin Joe taught her to fall into their arms and sigh, "My hero." Even playing Monopoly with Malcolm was more fun than usual; he and her brother Adriaan added bank robberies, high-speed chases, and full-out tackles — they called it "Full-Contact Monopoly." Malcolm even taught her essential life skills like shuffling and stacking a deck of cards like a pro. At thirteen, his imagination was fully intact. He created a new world for his cousins, adventures involving the rescue of kidnapped royalty. Together they fought goblins and dragons, leaped over fire, explored dangerous dungeons.

*

I WANTED MALCOLM to keep up his Nova Scotian connection. We sent him down for a stay with John and Celia, Nathan and Duncan. It was a satisfying trip but it prompted a deluge of tears because he'd heard the orchard on our former Hardwood Hill farm was being cut down so a logging road could be put through it. Some of those trips to the Maritimes were troubling. Once when we sent him down to see Bill in Halifax, he managed to lose — likely in the airport waiting lounge — his jacket and the $40 in spending money I'd given him. Confessing this to me on the phone, he wept and could not be consoled.

*

IN A RIBBON-TIED binder Malcom put together an extended self-portrait, apparently a school assignment.

ALL ABOUT ME!
A PROJECT BY MALCOLM SUTHERLAND
GO AHEAD AND READ IT, SEE IF I CARE!

The jocular tone belied the fact he regarded his room and desk-top as exclusively personal space. He took the precaution of titling a wirebound notebook "DREAM LOG. DO NOT READ." Once Alison accidentally — she said accidentally — read a passage from a journal he'd left open. It described in some detail considerations involved in a forthcoming drug deal. She was alarmed. To me it read more like a piece of fiction or a fantasy. She confronted him. He denied dealing in drugs. His main reaction was fury his privacy had been invaded.

Overall, the dream log seemed pretty inoffensive.

From "All About Me":

> I am Malcolm Sutherland of Toronto — but I wasn't here always.
>
> At the age of three I moved from Toronto to Nova Scotia with my grand-mother on my dad's side. I then moved to Portugal for three months, moved back to Nova Scotia for four years. Then moved back to Toronto.
>
> Enough about these places. How about where I'm living now? My dad is named Fraser Sutherland; he's a poet and a writer. He's working on a dictionary. My mom's named Alison Sutherland, a librarian.
>
> (From the description of my parents you must think I'm obsessed with books, but I'm not. I play Dungeons and Dragons and I like to draw.)
>
> Oh yeah, I almost forgot, my pets — they're part of the family too. I have a standard poodle (which is not one of those little toy poodles). He's champagne coloured with a liver coloured nose which is a breeding error (he is a little bit ashamed about it so I won't go into details). I have two cats, Becky and Sally. They

are Nova Scotia barn cats and were born with hybrid vigour. They are six years old and still going strong.

He itemized pet peeves:

— little girls who think they're cute but aren't
— people who think when I'm mad I'm funny
— bumper stickers you can't read
— people who monopolize the remote
— people who tell anecdotes and mix up the facts to make it more interesting
— the Marineland commercial you can hear even when you mute the TV

*

A HIGH SCHOOL handout asked him to list likes and dislikes to make an "Interest Profile" that it linked to possible future jobs. Malcolm was interested in painting, drawing, design, and sculpture. No surprises there. He had no mechanical interests. "What Qualities Are Important to Me?" the handout asked.

Most Important: *Smart, happy, out-going, trustworthy, creative*
Least important: *care-free, well-organized*
Name two things you do well: *drawing, painting*
Name your greatest success in life to date: *improving in math*
Name two things you would like to do better: *soccer, swimming*
Name one goal you would like to accomplish this year: *learn to fence*

Write three words that you would like said about you:
intelligent, talented, funny
Name the three people who have most influenced your
life: *Mom, Dad, Uncle Bill*

He was asked to rank values. He asked of friends that they be "Friendly, Sincere, Intelligent, Cheerful, Considerate, Talkative, Adventurous, Attractive." Of himself, he asked that he be "Fair, Sensible, Responsible, Outgoing, Intelligent, Friendly, Sincere, Honest."

*

SONHANDO, THE STEPSON of Malcolm's godfather, Adrian, was getting married in Manhattan. It would be good for Malcolm, I thought, to feel the rush of New York, cultural centrifuge and cyclotron, the capital of many worlds. Sonhando's wedding was unmissable. When he was very small his American mother Luci had brought him to Montreal and he had grown up a Montrealer, though she made sure he retained his U.S. citizenship. In Montreal she met Adrian. Luckily for both of them, he and Sonhando took to each other. In wedding Adrian she had married, in effect, a decrepit Chinese laundry that became what I considered the best little used-and-antiquarian bookshop in the country. It was my headquarters and my mail drop during the years I lived in the city.

Sonhando, the happy result of Luci's marriage to a Jamaican jazz musician, was a gifted marimba player, a percussionist graduate of the Berkeley School of Music in Boston. Although vibes was his specialty, he could play, as his mother said, anything he could hit with his hands or a stick. He plied the perilous trade of bicycle courier in Paris, and then in Manhattan. I imagined it was in Boston he met his bride, Patty. I didn't know what Patty's family, who appeared to be lace-curtain Irish, would make of the motley crew of Canadian family and friends they were about to encounter.

It was gloomy dark November but Malcolm, Alison, and I enjoyably killed time ducking in and out of museums before the wedding and reception in the back terrace of a restaurant. On a crowded subway car Alison and I squabbled about whether we were heading for or coming from uptown, midtown, or downtown. Speaking out of a deep well of experience Malcolm broke in, "You two are the most embarrassing people I've ever travelled with."

*

NOW THAT MALCOLM had entered his teens, Bill had taken it upon himself to offer sage, if shouted, advice to his MSPN about shaving and matters of personal hygiene. I didn't know how seriously Malcolm took the advice because he was already careful about how he looked. Perhaps, as with all his advice, it said more about Bill than about him. Separately came a little leather case containing "some tangible symbols of transition from childhood to young adulthood": a razor, deodorant, toothbrush, mouth spray, fingernail clipper, cuticle cutter, comb, shampoo. All had detailed instructions about use. He ended, "AVOID AT ALL COSTS BEING PHOTOGRAPHED WITH A DRINK, CIGARETTE OR YOUR DICK IN YOUR HAND. PHOTOGRAPHS HAVE LONG MEMOIRIES!"

*

THE PROUD, MODERATELY affluent protective parents of Malcolm's Grade Ten class organized an escorted if-it's-Tuesday-it-must-be-Naples tour of Italy. We really couldn't afford to send Malcolm on it, but peer pressure made us pony up. One technologically adept father set up a spot on the Web where the kids could post their tourist photos. He ensured nothing the kids did in public, no vista they witnessed, would go unrecorded and unpreserved, their every step electronically logged. I wondered if any bedroom farces were taking places in the students' hotels.

At the airport, Malcolm was stricken with a severe case of traveller's anxiety. As I often did under the same circumstances, he constantly patted his abdomen in case his passport had scuttled out of his money belt. Sleepless, after the flight he and his class were bussed to the ruins of Herculaneum, followed by Cumae. When parted from his classmates, he claimed to find shades and forms from long ago and the echo of voices. Mostly he held court to scuttling lizards. The tour guide lady chastised him, saying he didn't come to Italy to watch lizards. But watching lizards was exactly why he wanted to travel: he didn't need a guide, he thought, to tell him what to get out of a place.

The class went on to Rome and the Vatican, then Siena, where the cathedral's black-and-white pillars made him think it belonged to the movie *Beetlejuice*. In Florence he couldn't figure out why a cathedral would be built on a pagan site. In Verona they were told yet again the story of Romeo and Juliet. "To me," he wrote, "the story has very little to do with love. It is the story of violence, hatred, and adolescent angst." Apart from the stench of the canals, Venice was the city he'd choose to live in if he had the choice. He wondered that there were so many masks in sight, especially considering it was past Mardi Gras.

After Italy's charming lizards, its superior pizza and ice cream, its sunwarmed hills and echoing ruins, he was left with an Italian flu. On the plane ride back to Toronto he convulsed with shivering even though he was wearing three layers of clothing and was nestled between two other students. Even then he wasn't sure if he was conscious or in another dimension. It seemed seconds since their departure from Rome but hours since his last sip of orange juice. These reflections he put in the diary that Mr. M., his homeroom teacher, had obliged him to keep. Mr. M. sourly noted, "I'm sure you had more impressions than you remember." He gave the diary the mark of thirteen out of twenty.

*

WE PLAYED BACKGAMMON every evening, and tried out a new Monopoly board. Malcolm mourned the death by cat of Timothy, his second pet mouse. We buried Timothy next to Richard in the back garden.

He seemed to have lots of friends. He told one of them, Drazen, the son of Serbian immigrants, that life and reality are intertwined, so the energies flow from one to the other. Drazen may not have known what he meant but it sounded impressive.

As concerned dating, his school experience contrasted with mine. People didn't pair off as they had done when I was a teenager. Instead, someone would phone to ask if Malcolm wanted to go to a club, say, or a vacant stretch of lakeshore, ideal for a druggy hyperkinetic rave. A proposal would soon involve other people. Someone would suggest that someone else might join them. This required hanging up and making another call. Soon a whole chain of calls over cellphones ensued, each eliciting a positive or negative response. Eventually a core group would form. When Malcolm and his friends went to a club or a movie or a concert, they never went alone or with one other person. They went together by a process of agglutination, developing into a clot or clump.

Malcolm's generation seemed to me directionless, unmotivated, ambitionless, lacking any sense of where they wanted to go, or what they wanted to do once they got there. As the old rueful song or saying went, "What's the matter with kids today?" Why couldn't they be perfect, like we were? Although I had known while very young what I wanted to do with my life — I wanted to be a writer — I had no clear idea of how to go about it. Or how to go about sex. When sex surfaced in the course of dating, Malcolm's coevals seemed much saner than my cohort when suffering from the hormonal life-cycle disease called adolescence. Sex was no mystery to them; they'd got rudimentary sex education in the classroom — not that theory or anatomy lessons bore much relation to actuality. But there appeared to be no anguished ignorance or frustrated backseat fumblings. It seemed just a matter of getting it over with. Being obsessed with someone was seemingly frowned upon, though it was important to have a boyfriend or a girlfriend. Malcolm evidenced a certain ruthlessness in such matters. He had told me that, realizing for social reasons he should have a girlfriend, he had settled on someone, a voluble girl whose stepfather was the front man in a heavy-metal band. She was willing to be his steady. Wide-hipped and sturdy, Ashley had once been a hockey goaltender. It was easy to see how she could block the net. "That girl took my virginity," he later reflected, half proudly, half ruefully. At the time she had conflicts with her mother. I often heard Malcolm on the phone, quietly earnestly counselling her.

*

MY FATHER WAS hardly an alcoholic, but he didn't handle alcohol well when he did drink, and Alison's father undoubtedly drank too much, though not destructively. I began to wonder if Malcolm shared such tendencies. When we went to a mortgage-burning party in a friend's backyard, he made himself a cocktail from the several bottles on offer. Once he arrived back from a camping trip to find himself in the middle of a party I'd thrown together. While I was otherwise occupied, he guzzled drink. I later checked his whereabouts and found him lying in bed, stertorously breathing. As he grew older, he became a heroic, locomotive-style snorer like my father, my brother, and me. Alison once asked him if my snoring from our bedroom next to his bothered him. "No," he said, "I find it kind of friendly and comforting."

His alcoholic lapse was disquieting, but as near as I could make out his drinking was confined to an occasional beer. What he certainly did was smoke dope. Alison was implacably set against it, I was laissez-faire. Smoking dope was a way of life for teenagers. I didn't see how inveighing against it would do much good. My mother's inveighing against alcohol hadn't kept me from abusing it at times, or my brother from becoming an alcoholic. So I let Malcolm nurture a potted marijuana plant in the backyard; in a closet in his room he jerry-rigged a bright light to aid photosynthesis. It was a modest domestic grow-op. As a school assignment he mounted a rather solemn and stiff defence of dope smoking.

Why Marijuana Should Be Legalized
Cannabis Sativa. Marijuana. Pot. Grass. Weed. Ganja. Puff the magic dragon. This strange and misunderstood herb goes by many names, some may be common to you others may not. What comes to mind when I say these words?

Perhaps an addict lying in a puddle of vomit? Perhaps a dying aids patient at last finding a way to ease the pain. Perhaps a memory of a party you attended. Some of you have tried it. More of you have seen it. All of you have heard of it. It surrounds us every way we turn. We can't escape it. We *can* ignore it. We *can* fight against it, but no matter how hard we fight it is always a losing battle. It will always be there. Because it's popular and has been for over a thousand years. Its popularity will never fade and it will never go away not matter how harsh a penalty we impose on its users.

Is marijuana evil? Evil is too vague a word. Is marijuana harmful to us? Yes it's harmful if inhaling carbon, ash, and vegetable matter into our lungs is harmful. It causes cancer in the lungs like tobacco. It causes bronchitis. It's harmful to us if possession of this strange and misunderstood herb can result in five years or more in a jail cell. It's harmful if it becomes the most important aspect in our lives like alcohol to an alcoholic. So yes, in these ways it can be harmful.

What if it is? That argument hasn't stopped us with tobacco and alcohol. They cause as much if not more damage than marijuana. People are legally allowed to cause physical harm to themselves with these substances so why not pot? Why harass grass. Why ban ya ganja?

Marijuana kills brain cells. Marijuana is more addictive than tobacco. Heard of these sayings? They have been proved scientifically and by numerous studies to be incorrect.

Marijuana makes you lazy and takes away your work ethic. Marijuana is the reason communism doesn't work. Marijuana is the reason young people today are going to the dogs. Marijuana gives way to heavier drugs like heroin, crack and cocaine. If marijuana was legalised we would all spend all our time being high and living off welfare. Heard of these sayings? Are *they* true? Can *they* be scientifically confirmed or proven incorrect? No. Of course not. They're subjective and yet, *these* are the reasons that pot is illegal.

I'm not arguing that marijuana should be used. I'm not arguing it shouldn't. I'm arguing that rational adults should have the right to chose. Keep the age restrictions that apply to alcohol and tobacco in place for pot but legalise it. More lives have been ruined from the penalties that surround the use of marijuana than the effects of the drug itself ever have. Give the people of Canada the right to choose. Legalise marijuana.

Less preachy, though still solemn, was a school essay he wrote about a neighbourhood shop, "The Occult Shoppe, Vaughan's Pagan Oasis." He wrote that

the store's bleak and weatherworn front seems strangely comfortable nestled next to a stately apartment building and a fortune-teller's residence. A merry shrine of Hermes (for those who are mythologically challenged, the Greek god of messengers, athletes, thieves and trade) looks out on the street with strangely comforting eyes. In a way this prepares you for the interior, a sanctuary for both the wiccan (modern day witch) and the magickally (*k* left in to distinguish ceremonial magick from stage magic) inclined.

As you enter the shop a serendipitous aroma that seems to cling to one long after exiting greets you as new age music plays softly in the background. When you enter pause to take in your surroundings. On the north wall: shelves upon shelves of archaic looking herbs and oils. Separating you from the mysterious substances are cases containing tarot cards, divination kits, crystal balls, semi-precious stones, and my favourite items ... swords and daggers.

To the south, books on meditation, tantric sex rituals, astral projection, wicca, and of course magick, not to mention incense of every shape and smell. Straight-ahead candles line neat aisles alongside ritual bath equipment and home-made blackberry ink.

I find the staff helpful (if condescending) and the merchandise fairly comprehensive. Workers will enthusiastically answer any politely phrased questions, even those philosophical in nature, one even took the time for a brief interview. She seemed a little suspicious of the tape recorder, probably because of the bad press wiccans have been getting over the years. After reading my questions she decided I was on her side and we commenced with the interview. At one point he asked, motioning to an amber statuette seated among bowls of herbs, cigars, and pennies, "Who is this behind you?"

"That's Oshun (Ō 'Shŭn), she's an African goddess, godess of fertility, love, money, jewels, gold, beauty, very friendly, but if you piss her off you're in for trouble."

"How do you piss her off?"

"Steal from the shrine."

"What advice would you give to young people today interested in pursuing the wiccan path?"

"Read as much as you can. Even about different pantheons that were into a nature based religion. If you don't know the meaning of a symbol or word or name find out as much as you can before you use it because there's a lot of power in different things. The wicca religion is mostly white magick it only deals with positive energy."

"What makes white magick, white magick?"

"Okay, White Magick. A lot of people like to say 'White magick' or 'Black magick,' me personally I feel that there is not really either one but there is grey magick and different tones of it. You are using white magick if you are not trying to control or manipulate others. We don't sacrifice animals in any bloodthirsty way. When you do a spell you are working with your own energy, enhancing the world around you. You can't just do magick, you need to have the belief, the knowledge and the will."

"Thank you for your time."

"No problem."

The occult shop, he wrote,

> is the kind of place I can get lost in. Its atmosphere makes you want to lower your voice out of respect for whatever unseen forces may be at work within its esoteric walls. Be sure to check it out, who knows? You may just find that something inside calls to you from outside our mundane reality.

He didn't actually specify what he bought at the shop. In fact, I'm not sure he bought anything there but incense. But he did take the occult seriously. Still, satire was second nature to him, likely borrowed from me, or so I flattered myself. He was addicted to *The Simpsons*. Which cartoon character did he identify with, I wondered — the irrepressible Bart Simpson maybe, or perhaps the crusty Krusty the Clown? Foreign-language soap operas on TV gave him a chance to dub zany dialogue. He was a maestro of phone stunts. One favoured victim was a diet-plan outfit called Jenny Craig, whose TV commercials plagued the airwaves. On a bus platform at a subway station, he would commandeer two pay phones. He would dial Jenny Craig on both phones, complaining he was fat and ugly and had pimples and nobody loved him. That was what he reported he'd said. Somehow he contrived it, or at least said he did, that two Jenny Craig operators would end up shouting at each other.

Knowing his special talent, I would always hand him the phone whenever a pestiferous telemarketer called. Someone who, say, wanted to sell us aluminum-frame windows would be closely questioned. "Does the aluminum cover the windows?" he would ask.

"Yes."

"Then how do you see out?"

Someone would phone, ostensibly taking a survey about motor vehicles.

"Do you have a motor vehicle in your household?"

"Yes," Malcolm would answer.

Was it a car? No. A truck? No, An SUV? No.

Long pause: the questioner was puzzled. Malcolm helped him out.

"… But we have a hovercraft."

*

MALCOLM NEVER CEASED probing his interior life. "A lucid dream," he wrote. "I dream within the main dream. Flute music is playing, and I am hanging on to a rope of some sort and being swung over the green hills. I wondered since it is a dream what would ever happen if I let go. I did, and I fell. I hit the ground and rolled, the world was spinning round and round and I landed with a thud in my dream-bed." Lisa Simpson of The Simpsons, Bart's sister, figured: "Finally I realized that Lisa Simpson was a fictional character so that must be a dream. She nodded understandingly as if I had just grasped the concept."

Malcolm's penchant for subversive mischief erupted one late spring day. It led to getting suspended from school. During a class visit to the Pine River Outdoor Education Centre, he tampered with the toilets so they splashed back when flushed.

No doubt because he was ordered to, he wrote a detailed exegesis of what he had done, and what he had been thinking when he did it.

When I went to the Pine River school I had an idea for a practical joke. I got the idea when I removed the back of one of the toilets (I lifted the lid on the back). I then lifted the tube where I saw the toilet was filled from and saw water would shoot out from this whenever the toilet was flushed. I pointed this out of the toilet and replaced the lid. I did the same to the other three. I then left the bathroom. I forgot about the toilets until the next day. I entered to use the facilities. I noticed the tube was no longer pointing out of the lid. I thought maybe the tube had slipped back inside. I reset the tube and left.

Later when I was in the common room my science teacher instructed all the boys to stand outside the washroom. She said that the person who confessed to the prank would have to clean the washroom and the rest would be left off the hook. I did not confess. The science teacher then said if someone did not confess by the end of the day the students would have no free time for movies, and would have to do a science assignment. By this time the students were shouting and yelling for someone to confess. I should have confessed now but I didn't have the courage to stand up to the witch-hunt that had grown up around the incident.

We were dismissed to the next activity and I tried to look for a time when the science teacher would be alone to confess. But every time I tried she was always with other students. I know this is no excuse. I just wanted to keep it between myself and the Pine River staff. After the activity I found the Vaughan math teacher and confessed to him and apologized for not confessing earlier. I felt an enormous sense of relief to get what I thought was a stupid little secret off my back.

When the science teacher returned I accompanied her to the office of the Pine River vice principal. I apologized to him and the caretaker who had to clean up after me …

He was told to list the problems his practical joke caused. He did that, concluding,

My behaviour was inconvenient, mean, and thoughtless because I failed to consider the ramifications of my action on myself and others.

Over the past week I have been thinking about my actions and I have been, frankly, scared stiff. All I can say in my defence is that in performing the practical joke I tried not to do damage to the toilets in question. From what I have been told there were no damages aside from the floor being flooded twice, wasted toilet paper and a lot of work for the Pine River that could have been avoided had I shown more consideration about my actions.

Second, I am for the most part unable to discern what a suitable punishment should be for my action. I can only offer one idea: an additional apology to the Pine River staff and time spent performing janitorial service at Vaughan so I can learn what it is like to be in the caretaker's shoes who had to clean up after my action. This will not help the staff at Pine River who had to clean up after me but it will keep me from doing something so thoughtless, stupid, and inconsiderate again.

The explanation, suspension, and janitorial tasks weren't the end of it. He was also compelled to write an apology to the Pine River supervisor. "I'm not brown-nosing, I mean that Vaughan is an okay school and unless its reputation has been tarnished before I came don't let my stupidity ruin your opinion of it."

*

THAT SUMMER HE made excursions, with me to Nova Scotia and alone to Victoria. On New Year's Day, after one of his beach raves, I took him to see the Coen brothers' *O Brother, Where Art Thou?* The movie was great. On our way home we stopped at a Chinese supermarket. Suddenly Malcolm began to shake and shudder, his feet beating a tattoo. I wondered whether this was St. Vitus dance. Should I get him to a hospital's emergency ward? Was this uncontrolled jig an aftermath of ecstasy, "E," a favourite recreational drug of his set? Or something else? To my great relief the jig abruptly ended.

*

WE HAD BEGUN to scout where he might go to university. He applied to several. His marks were good, though not nearly as good as those of a blond Russian girl who swept all before her with multiple scholarships. He won a Lions Club bursary but neglected to write a thank-you letter to the donor, which earned him a sharp rebuke in the form of a phone call from the man, who was under no illusion virtue should be its own reward. He won a trophy for the highest standing in art. He won scholarships to two universities, one on the Toronto outskirts, one in a nearby city, but chose a third, the most prestigious.

Trinity, a federated college of the University of Toronto, was by way of being an Anglican family enterprise. Alison and many of her cousins had gone there, a forbear had endowed a tower in its quadrangle, an uncle and his father had been its provosts, and the latter had been the Anglican Archbishop of Canada. I wished Malcolm would escape the Toronto scene entirely and go somewhere like the small Mount Allison University in the Maritimes, but we couldn't afford it. True, he'd had savings from years of summer or part-time jobs, such as one at a greengrocer's a few blocks away, memorable to me because his boss referred to a variety of cucumbers he sold as "girly cukes." But, savings or scholarships aside, the choice seemed almost inevitable: he could live at home and make the short commute to classes.

He didn't resist any pressures about following a family tradition. He embraced tradition. He was drawn to rituals, ceremonies, tribal customs. Trinity College seemed to offer them, a pocket of WASP ethnicity, another ethnicity in a city that had so many of them. It was a pity that we couldn't afford to have him stay in residence. He embarked on his freshman week with great enthusiasm, even to calmly accepting the hazing of Frosh Week in which he was forced to drink a vomitous mixture, and was dropped off out of town and required to make his own way back. He joined Trinity's black-gowned choir: he couldn't read music, but a resonant bass voice like his was in demand.

As it turned out, Trinity College was not really a bastion of tribalism. It was a nearly indistinguishable link in a corporate multiversity in which the identity of each college was firmly quelled or quenched as soon as it seemed likely to be asserted.

*

MALCOLM HAD BEEN spending a lot of time with a new friend. Five years older, Blaine had a resounding First Nations surname. He was slim, pale, close-cropped, and lived with his sister in a cheap apartment. He was having a heavy-duty dispute with his landlord about plumbing, or the lack of it. Malcolm often spent overnight at his place. I wondered what went on, but drugs or drink didn't seem to be part of it. Rather, he and Blaine appeared to spend their time inchoately dreaming and scheming.

Blaine, who had drawing talent, sketched on a piece of paper a shopping centre to rise on a plot of land he said he owned outside Cambridge, a small city a hundred kilometres west. Where the money for its construction was going to come from I didn't know: it certainly wasn't going to come from Malcolm, or from me. When he showed us the plans spread out on our dining-room table, I was carefully noncommittal. Perhaps aware that we feared he was exploiting Malcolm, he politely said that this real estate developer's initiative was Malcolm's, not his.

As time went on, Blaine got interested in the thirty-acre Nova Scotia woodlot my mother had bequeathed to her only grandson. On this site, he and Malcolm thought, an amusement park could be erected. They drafted an agreement, according to which Malcolm gave him permission to erect "structures." Now, abandoning their ruinous apartment, he and his sister — *was* she his sister? — journeyed to Nova Scotia. In midwinter they erected a tent in the forest snowdrifts, puzzling the young farmer who owned the adjacent woodlot. The camping couple soon joined the Pictou County welfare rolls before returning to Toronto. A change from the old pattern of down-and-out Maritimers joining the Toronto welfare rolls.

Whether it was due to an emerging conflict or just gradual disillusionment, Malcolm became disabused with Blaine. He began to ask me what I thought of him. I candidly but cautiously — I'd long maintained a hands-off policy about his choice of friends — said I thought he was a taker, not a giver. Malcolm stopped seeing him; to my relief the overnighters ended. Later, Malcolm told me he'd been involved with Blaine's sister. Perhaps this was a partial clue to the seemingly odd relationship. Another one was that for years to come every night he made sure our house's front and back doors were locked before he went to bed.

*

AS IT HAPPENED, Blaine aroused long-distance enmity in conservative Bill, who wrote that Blaine was obviously "a loser." This led to my telling him: "Losers are often more interesting, and more fun to be with, than winners. To say so reflects my bias as a writer, because losers make for great material." I thought that something like that might account for Malcolm's attraction to Blaine, because Malcolm delighted in telling me about all the things that had gone wrong, some of them quite bizarre, in Blaine's life. Blaine was a fabulist (a liar, to Bill) and a dreamer, for sure. But he'd always been honest financially in his business or quasi-business dealings with Malcolm (jewelry-making, getting him a CD drive), though sometimes tardy in meeting his obligations. When Malcolm told me that they had decided to be friends and not business partners, I breathed a sigh of relief.

I wrote Bill that Malcolm was "fiercely loyal to his friends. And he's told us that making the land agreement was a way of asserting his independence. I can understand that. He leads a somewhat sheltered and oversupervised existence (we don't interfere with his social life but just the same we're around all the time) living at home as an only child. He wanted to make his own decisions, even if they were wrong ones." Actually owning some land gave him a bit of power in a generally powerless life.

One decision he made was to enthusiastically join the Ommies. They took their name from *Om*, the mystic Sanskrit syllable in *Om mani padme hum*. Jewel in the lotus, the Buddhist sacred flower, the spirit of enlightenment. Not exactly a cult or movement, more a tendency, the Ommies of Toronto symbolized or personified the New Age spectrum of crystals, energy-field auras, alternative spirituality, environmentalism, and holism. Most of the people were his own age, or a bit older. The same magnetic attraction drew him to Indigenous drumming circles in a downtown park; from his room came the sound of bongos. The Ommies, and the music they favoured, took him by car pool to country weekends far north of the city. He stoutly denied these excursions had anything to do with drugs: they were all about the music. At one of these weekends he fell in love with a girl with red-gold hair, Krista. He described how they had reached a mystic communion in which they had exchanged ectoplasm or something as sublimely vital, which, Alison snorted, was more likely LSD.

The girl was fond of him, but she was a bit older. I surmised she had other romantic interests, and in any event she was going to attend university in British Columbia. First love led to first loss.

He had friends his own age, he had cousins about the same age, but he didn't have brothers or sisters. He was acquiring the qualities attributed to singletons. Thrown among adults from birth, beginning with his parents, he always seemed older, more mature and articulate, more polite, than children his own age. His best friends were oldest children or singletons like himself. He had specialized solitary interests and pastimes. He had no interest in politics, though he did volunteer that our Black female governor general, Michaëlle Jean, a former broadcast journalist, was "hot." He liked to dance to the hypnotic, pounding music that leaked out of his bedroom, or retreat into the abstracted displacement of meditation, of which he was doing more and more.

In *The Drawing Master*, a documentary film about the chairman of my Tuesday night beer-drinking circle, Malcolm is seen in the midst of a happy swilling crowd of adults. Away from my friends, Malcolm's intense interior life went on. Mystical mantras were chanted, white-magic spells enacted behind his closed bedroom door. He was taking courses in philosophy and religion, but the detailed copious notes he made in his journals came from his own sources.

*

IN THE PART of the house outside his room it was part of our domestic economy that no policy or practice could go unchallenged, at least by me. Alison and Malcolm were always hanging lumpy woolly sweatshirts with parkas on the pegs near the front door, shapeless fuzzballs that were always falling to the floor. I never saw them wear these garments. They accumulated like lint. Every time I entered or exited the house they were there, not so much begging to be worn as smugly dangling. We had no air conditioning, so we had an ongoing debate about whether opening or closing the front and back doors made it hotter inside the house. Malcolm argued that closing them made it cooler; I argued that it didn't.

The triviality of our debates was unlimited. I always twisted the cap on a toothpaste tube back on when I found it off. He would argue that keeping the cap separate from the tube eliminated the bother of always putting it on again. I argued keeping the cap off led to the cap's being misplaced or lost, and dried out the toothpaste. He countered that squeezing the tube several times a day prevented its drying out.

I could see behind such controversies was a principle. His was that things should be open, mine that they should be closed.

*

ALISON AND I had suspicions and anxieties about what he was up to behind his closed door, especially when he had guests. But we felt confident enough about his trustworthiness to go on a holiday to New Orleans, my favourite American city. While we were away he was to perform all the chores I typically did: take Julius, our latest poodle, on a walk around the block twice a day; feed the ancient Becky and Barnaby, the feisty Burmese we'd acquired not long after moving in. Malcolm was required to empty a waste bin into the composter, to put throwaway glass and plastic into the Blue Box. TV-type dinners were in the fridge's freezer compartment. Mornings, he was to take in the newspaper from the porch. He was to feed the animals on demand, and turn off all lights in rooms when leaving the house, as well as lock all doors. He was to replace toilet paper on the roller if finished. He was to water plants on the porch on sunny days (in the evening). There were a few prohibitions. He was not to

1. Undertake extensive interior decoration of his room with the help of guests. (This stricture alluded to the time some of his pals had arrived late at night to repaint his room.)
2. To place, or have a guest place, large, heavy objects in high or unstable positions.
3. To cook large, or any other, meals by candlelight. (Another regrettable moment in the past.)

4. To leave a pot or pan on the stove unattended.
5. To leave Barnaby unsupervised in the backyard, or
    to leave the house without making sure Barnaby and
    Julius were inside.

Otherwise, he was to have fun.

*

MALCOLM HAD HIS self-indulgences, but he also showed powers of empathy with a surprising range of sentient creatures. Once he came up to my office, a tiny bird cupped in his hands. He had found it passed out on the sidewalk. It took some phoning but I was able to identify it as a golden-crowned kinglet. It was one of the most beautiful of small perching birds. I didn't know what to do with the damn thing as it flew around my office. When I tried to free it from between two panes of glass I gashed my hand on the window frame. We managed to get it corralled into a cat carrier — minus a cat, of course. We released it in the backyard so it could fly to Guatemala.

*

ONE EVENING MALCOLM came downstairs and asked me to look at his eyes. Indeed, his pupils were hugely dilated. He told me he and Adrian had chewed magic mushrooms. I phoned Adrian's father Bruce, who drove us down to the Toronto General's emergency department. No one there seemed to think it was much of an emergency. Jolly Adrian didn't appear to take it seriously. No lasting harm seemed to have been done.

*

AFTER MALCOLM BEGAN at Trinity he was lauded, along with a lot of others, at Vaughan Road Academy's commencement ceremony. In the program the graduates contributed brief statements about themselves. Malcolm's: "Malcolm Sutherland is studying philosophy at the University of Toronto. His employer is the High Priest of the Kingdom of Nod." I told him I thought he was being silly.

*

IN EARLY DECEMBER of that first Trinity year he reported that he'd lost a pair of glasses. During the fall he'd also lost, at minimum, two overcoats and a portfolio case. It was as if he never wanted to keep anything, like a mendicant attached only to his begging bowl. "When was the last time you used it?" I would ask about some missing object. I would tell him to think of an object like a wallet or a wristwatch as part of his body, some vital organic part of his person. His sheepishness was matched by my disgust. I angrily quoted the homely saying of a Dutch neighbour back in Nova Scotia: "You'd lose your ass if it wasn't attached to you."

He was the least materialistic kid I'd ever encountered. With rare exceptions, losing possessions didn't seem to bother him. He never wore a wristwatch, a custom he'd inherited from Alison, like dropping clothes on the floor when he went to bed. But the lack of a wristwatch never kept her from keeping appointments, and in fact he usually didn't miss lectures or exams. Maybe he didn't need a watch. Maybe it signified he lived in a timeless universe.

PART THREE

S UMMER WAS COMING to an end, and so was the latest of
Malcolm's part-time jobs — so many of them in so few
years — this one as an oddsbody at the Canada's Wonderland
entertainment park north of downtown. That summer he'd also
taught art to kids for the city's parks and recreation department,
and done night shifts as a security guard at a pop concert, though it
was hard to imagine Malcolm with the ruthless muscle to security-
guard anything.

He had something on his mind, it seemed to me. A stranger,
an unassuming but suspiciously friendly guy about his age, had
came round to see him one afternoon. They closeted themselves
in Malcolm's bedroom. I had a very bad feeling about this smiling
polite stranger. I couldn't locate the source of this disquiet. A dope
pusher? Maybe. I didn't act on my suspicions. What was there to

intervene about, and why shouldn't Malcolm make friends with anyone he wanted? I went for a nervous solitary walk, leaving them alone.

In the following week, Malcolm wasn't his usual cheerful self. When my old friend Adrian from Montreal came to move his son's furniture stored in our basement, Malcolm sat in his bathrobe in the backyard, not offering to help, abstracted, dulled and feverish, as if he had the flu. He had in fact a low fever, and didn't attend a pal's birthday party. About this time Monique, the woman with whom I once lived in Montreal, arrived from her permanent residence in the Indian Himalayas. He emerged from his fugue long enough to discuss meditation practices.

After she left, he bitterly resisted Alison's nagging him to help out with household chores like washing dishes. He'd not always been a willing helper but this was nothing like a normal domestic row. He raised a series of tense legalistic objections. We settled he would make a meal now and then. So that night he made dinner: routine hamburger patties, mushy boiled potatoes, watery broccoli.

He'd been listless all week, and I couldn't coax him to a baseball game for which I'd been given tickets. He spent long hours in his room meditating, sometimes lying flat, sometimes sitting cross-legged. He walked stiffly, laughing at nothing, an odd smile on his face, a time lag between a remark made to him and his response to it. But most of the time he seemed just as he usually was.

But something was happening in his life, and I didn't know what it was. He went to the University of Toronto campus to unravel red tape about his forthcoming semester.

*

A CLOSE FRIEND was in crisis. Fred, who was dating Malcolm's former girlfriend and schoolmate Ashley, had a psychotic breakdown.

His mania took the form of a Christ complex. Trying to re-enact Christ's sacrifice, he scarred his arms and legs with a knife. Malcolm felt guilty he had not informed Ashley or Fred's father of the delusion, though surely they would have known anyway. For the time being Fred was in "the Clarke," short for the Clarke Institute of Psychiatry, housed in a high-rise egg carton near the corner of College and Spadina. The Clarke was an outpost of CAMH, the Centre for Addiction and Mental Health, the largest mental-health teaching hospital in the country. Malcolm went to visit him. They played chess.

Late one morning, working in my office, I heard Malcolm take a shower in the bathroom next door. Then a series of thumps and a crash. I discovered him at the top of the stairs, apparently about to throw himself down them. At least that seemed to be what he was trying to do. Bumping down the stairs on his buttocks, a big bump for each tread. He looked at once frozen and terrified. Was launching himself from the top of the stairs an attempt at suicide? I coaxed him to sit on his bed, talked to him. I asked him whether he was upset about Fred. He said that was it. I tried to comfort him. I am not a huggy person but I hugged him. He sobbed. He seemed to identify with Fred. At the same time he wanted to "connect" with something, that hurting himself felt good, or at least "interesting."

I left him. A few minutes later I heard the alarming ridiculous bumps again. I recalled how, when he was little, Alison would gather up the laundry and strew it on the stairs, to be stuffed into a bundle buggy and lugged off to the Laundromat. Malcolm would climb aboard the pile of clothes and coast down the stairs. I called it "riding the high laundry."

There was no laundry now, only this mad bump, bump, bump down the steps. I pleaded with him to stop. At intervals he did. When Alison returned from work I took her out to sit on the porch steps, telling her what had happened.

That day was the registration deadline for enrolment at Trinity College. He taxied with Alison to the campus. En route he slapped his face. When they got back she phoned the United Church of Canada headquarters where she was a studio administrator in the resource production wing, a job she'd begun a year earlier. The church had a phone therapist on tap. Malcolm talked to him. On the therapist's advice we called a cab to go to a hospital. He began punching himself in the face. With him sandwiched between us in the back seat, we headed off on the short, long trip to the Mount Sinai Hospital emergency ward.

We waited for several hours, first for a triage nurse, then to be seen by a doctor. He kept trying to hit himself while I fiercely murmured, "Don't, Malcolm, *don't*!" I devoutly wished this self-hurting would end, even more that it had never started. At last we were admitted to a populated sanctum. He sat in an examining room, recalcitrant. He stuffed Kleenex in his mouth and chewed it. "Don't, Malcolm, don't!" I protested. He consented to an EKG and a blood test, but adamantly refused to take a urine test or an Ativan pill a nurse offered him. Ativan was used to treat anxiety. After much coaxing he suddenly relented about taking the urine test. He asked for a glass of water and upturned it on his head. When Alison offered him a Kleenex he furiously chewed it up and swallowed the shreds, glaring at her. I had no idea why his anger should settle on her.

The Mount Sinai staff were unable or unwilling to deal with his problems, so they referred him to CAMH's Clarke branch, dispatching someone to accompany us there on a brief taxi journey up University Avenue and along College Street, bordering his campus. Past the double-doored back entrance off the parking lot was a locked waiting room. A few people sat there, though it was hard to tell which were patients, which family or friends. Overhead a mute television was on, the channel or program unidentifiable.

Behind a big glass window were the professionals: nurses, doctors, and clericals, staring into computer monitors, filling out forms, for all we knew exchanging muffin recipes. At intervals, Malcolm tried to hit himself harder. A hospital-garbed man emerging from within the barricaded office said, "Let him do it." Malcolm was an attention-seeker, it seemed. I couldn't stand it and restrained him. He didn't fight me. From time to time I got permission to get a coffee or go out to the parking lot for a cigarette.

A young psychiatrist asked to see us alone. "Will he be OK alone?" we asked the staff. They said, "Oh, yes." We went off to see the doctor in a tiny, bare interview room. A knock on the door.

Malcolm had done something violent. We hurried down the hall. Malcolm had hit himself so hard one side of his head was swollen and one eye was closed. We waited tensely while a doctor checked the eye. He had not badly damaged himself.

What had happened precipitated action. He was going upstairs to the Acute Care Ward. We hugged him goodnight. It was 3:00 a.m.

*

THE ACW WAS a long, wide, locked-in corridor. Leading off it was the usual glassed-in office, a glassed-in cubicle for smokers, and a series of slots sheathed by curtains, each barely big enough to contain a bed. From behind the curtains came silence, or indecipherable babble. Some patients paced the corridor.

Malcolm was tied wrists and ankles to a bed in a cubicle. Unresponsive, groggy, he'd been forcibly injected with Ativan and Acuphase, an antipsychotic, having refused to take them orally. The black eye was less swollen and discoloured. A medical student interviewed us. Malcolm ate a bit of a snack I had brought him but, during supper, began to hit himself and had to be put back in restraints.

Days passed. Alison dropped in on Malcolm on her way home from work, or in the evening, alternating with the hours I saw him in the afternoons. We found him stretched out in his cubicle, laid low by massive doses of tranquilizers to keep him from "self-inflicting." Sometimes his wrists and ankles were bound with cloth. When he felt an attack coming on he'd ask for restraints. He was quiet and co-operative, weeping a little. As the nurse gently did up the straps, she said, "Malcolm, try to just relax and think of something absolutely wonderful …" He gradually relaxed as Alison sat beside him. He opened one eye, grinned, and said, "Do you want the bow or the stern?"

"Huh?" she said.

"The wonderful thing I am thinking about is being in a canoe at Go Home Bay."

The black bruise around his eye gradually faded, and the eye opened. There was another bruise, a long purple one along his flank I saw when I took him to a shower, the first one he'd had since he'd been admitted. Another sign of progress: he began to ask for clothes, shaving cream, and other personal items from home. But he was still in the "acute phase."

There was no chance he could start classes at the university now, or for the foreseeable future.

*

ABOUT THIS TIME his friend Fred was joined at the Clarke by his brother Phil, newly admitted with schizophrenia. It was a luckless family. When Alison and I saw Fred he seemed unnaturally sociable and cheerful. An intercepted letter from him to Malcolm began, "I'm sorry I got you in this mess." Was this some kind of psychotic homosexual pact, in which each of them decided to simultaneously go crazy? It seemed pretty unlikely. The rest of Fred's letter said that he planned to feign recovery and on release commit "legal suicide" in order to escape the grip of Satan.

Arriving at noon, I would bring Malcolm bean-curd treats from a nearby Vietnamese eatery. From Halifax, Bill phoned several times a week. I didn't tell him that on at least one occasion Malcolm had been found in the bathroom eating his feces. "I'm shit," he told the staff. "So why shouldn't I eat it?"

He'd leave his bed to have lunch at a corridor table. I had to watch him carefully because he was liable to dump a cup of fruit juice on his head, or anything at all, really: it could be soup, salad, or sunflower seeds. The same was true when we got a pass to take him out into daylight for a cup of tea. I would spot a telltale twitch as he reached for something to upturn. He said he found the reflex mysterious, frustrating, and very embarrassing: "I don't know why I do these stupid things."

He was shunted to the general psych ward, though it wasn't long before he went back to the ACU after going from bedroom to bathroom naked or taking off his clothing as he went. His friends came to visit, arousing our fears one might slip him drugs. Sneaking in drugs to patients was not unknown at the Clarke.

He gave himself an exercise regime of sit-ups and push-ups. He resisted being given pills, and sometimes had to be forcibly injected. He hated the way being medicated made him feel. Over- or undermedicated, he was still sharp-witted. When he reported that a friend named Ben had phoned, I said, "I'm confused. You know several Bens." He said, "Yeah. I'm going around the Ben."

*

TO VISIT MALCOLM was to watch him choose which liquid to pour on his head — tea or juice. We even invented a verb for it: "juicing." In the rudimentary diary he was keeping, he wrote, "Around 8, I poured juice on my head. Impulse ended. After, I felt embarrassed and wet, no relief." A few days later he anointed himself with soup, juice, and Jell-O, flowing into his T-shirt, puddling on the floor. But he reached a point at which he could ask a nurse to take a glass of juice away if it posed a threat.

There were also external threats. A male nurse muttered to me, "Keep his friends away from him."

On the Ommie social network he wrote, "Mom worries about me and likes to blame the drugs. I've been off them for a month! I say, 'Longer for pot.' But nevertheless she posts on the Om board. It's an odd message, I'm told, a weird mix of love, protection, and paranoia. She wants to know who is responsible for messing up her son's mind."

He concluded, "Her son is."

*

WE SAT IN the cosy cluttered office of Dr. S., supervisor of the Acute Care Ward, in charge of all the new-patient intake. That seemed to be a lot to take care of, but Dr. S. gave us his personal attention almost as soon as Malcolm was admitted. Diplomas and amateur artwork festooned his walls. He was bald, genial, Mexican in origin — the last predisposed him in my favour. He told us the Mount Sinai blood test had shown traces of amphetamines. Malcolm had repeatedly denied that he had taken any, though he'd told us that a month earlier he'd taken ecstasy that had traces of other amphetamines in it, presumably why the latter showed up in a test result. Dr. S. said that sometimes drugs could trigger a psychotic episode; it was hard to know whether this particular episode would be temporary or not. It would take time to find out.

He took notes about our family history. On Alison's side, her grandmother, a doctor's wife, had committed suicide, her father, a niece, and a cousin had attempted it, and so had she. A lot of chronic depression going around. I said I had often been depressed.

"Is there a history of depression in your family?"

"I'm a writer," I said.

Our sessions did not go smoothly. When Alison succumbed to tears of frustration, rage, or sorrow, Dr. S. was unsympathetic. We prepared a detailed chronology of what had happened to Malcolm before and during his admission, hoping it would provide context and guide treatment. Dr. S. sourly remarked it seemed "litigious." Suing anybody was far from our minds, we assured him. He probed Malcolm's upbringing, and asked emphatically, *"What is wrong with this family?"*

What was wrong with this family, I thought, was our son's psychosis. Because Malcolm seemed atypical, Dr. S. began to suggest he was faking. It took a lot of faking, I thought, to give oneself a black eye and eat one's own feces. When Malcolm sat in with us, Dr. S. asked him why he was behaving the way he was. Malcolm said he was "trying to get attention." It was like an answer that he'd come up with to placate whoever was asking.

He never explained, or rather he didn't know, from where the instructions or orders to say or do dreadful things came from, and whether they came as voices or just impulses. To me they were like phone calls from hell.

He was shifted across the hall to a ward where patients didn't act so dramatically on their impulses, or else were more heavily sedated. He got a pass, allowing him to go home overnight or on weekends. Alison set him to work washing the kitchen ceiling, and he did it dutifully, glumly. But his mind was elsewhere. Returning to the Clarke from one of these homecomings, he bumped down the steps of the back porch on his buttocks. He was shunted back to the ACW.

The times he was home, I would work in my office, my ears tuned to repeated thumps or a crash, which never failed to make me jump.

It was the signal he was bumping down the stairs, or had hit the bottom. I didn't have to be in the office, though; I could be reading a book in the living room and he would start bumping down, go back to the top, and start again. A Clarke psychiatrist said to just let him do it until he tired himself out, having failed in a bid to get attention. I wondered what he would say if Malcolm damaged his spine.

The passes to go home always led to entanglements. Often these involved taking along the right pills, or wondering when to take them. On the long Thanksgiving weekend he got a pass, but the Clarke staff neglected to give him an antipsychotic injection to tide him over. At home he promptly began to hit himself and hurl himself down the stairs.

Back in the Clarke he often emerged nude from his room. On one of these occasions, Alison cried, "Oh, Malcolm, for heaven's sake put on some clothes." He did. He started to disrobe on crowded street corners. Asked why, he gave the all-purpose explanation he did it to get attention. At the Clarke he was said to have urinated and defecated in bed. He wrote, "I don't know why this is happening," at the same time as he was trying to fob off his caregivers with his "I'm seeking attention" excuse. The psychiatrists who saw him called his problems "behavioural," not psychotic.

When he came home we gave him manageable chores, which he carried out quietly, obediently. A couple of days after he re-entered the Clarke, Dr. J., one of his psychiatrists, phoned to order me to remove him at once, since his objectionable behaviour had been disruptive to the staff. He was only regressing at the Clarke, the doctor said, and might do better at home. If necessary, he could be brought to the Clarke ER should a "life-threatening" situation occur at home. That was reassuring.

The professionals, it seemed, couldn't handle him. I went to fetch him. For the rest of October back and forth we went to the Clarke, and back and forth went our emails. There were slow, groggy days; occasionally there were hellish days like one late that month. That day at home he tried bumping down the stairs three times in a row before I stopped him. I worried that he might hurt himself with all his bumping down the stairs, but Dr. J., a Clarke psychiatrist, didn't share my concern.

There were struggles in our family doctor's waiting room and on the TTC en route to yet another unrewarding session with Dr. S. One day he got up early to slide and bump repeatedly. I ignored him. Julius, our latest poodle, didn't. One day I was reading a book in the living room when he did it ten times in a row at short intervals. I told him to go to his room, after which he came down and wanted to shave his head with dog clippers.

One day when he was back at the Clarke a Black nurse came to take blood samples. He grabbed at her buttocks and called her the N-word. This was shocking. Up to then it would have been impossible to imagine anyone less racist than he. Dr. S. gravely warned us Malcolm could face criminal charges for this kind of behaviour. Tough Love was in order. Dr. S. ordered him to write letters of apology to the nurse he had groped. Malcolm humbly wrote them. Following the script, I gave him a severe lecture when he came home on a pass. He didn't attempt to defend himself.

Soon I got a phone call from his social worker, who said he was being discharged to go a place of his own choosing — though not home. The psychiatrists were practising Tough Love all right. He chose, the social worker said, the Na-Me-Res, a residence for Indigenous men. If they aimed to give him a taste of independent living apart from his parents, this seemed counterproductive. The Na-Me-Res was only a short walk from our house; we passed it every day. Malcolm wasn't Indigenous. His choice was crazy. Even more certifiable was what the hospital was doing.

The staff, the ones we talked to anyway, had apparently concluded his behaviour was mere attention-seeking and our parenting skills were to blame. I told the social worker that if Malcolm were released on his own and harm came to him or anyone else, I would sue the hospital's ass off. It was not a threat, but a promise. Despair and desperation had forced me into this corner. The social worker wanted to transfer my call to a psychiatrist. I didn't want to be coated with a layer of bafflegab, or allow myself to be cowed by ostensibly authoritative professionals. The matter seemed simple to me. Malcolm was sick, and the hospital wasn't trying to cure him. I was ashamed and furious I'd followed its tough-love advice and upbraided him for bad behaviour. The poor bugger couldn't help it.

I told Alison what had happened. She shrieked at the CAMH staff that Malcolm had been fine until the first episode of hitting himself, and that if he was doing those horrible things purely for attention and IF the family was THAT toxic, there should have been evidence of it for years. "Talk to our family doctor!" she said. "Or his teachers, or any of his friends!" She supplied names and phone numbers.

Certainly, no one who had known Malcolm over many years could have imagined anyone less aggressive or racist. If he was dreamy, unambitious, and intermittently took street drugs, he was also the funniest, gentlest, smartest, most affectionate son anyone could wish for. Up to then, he had said that he'd been "seeking attention," but he now confessed that inner impulses had directed him. He'd never revealed this to the doctors before, never told them, they said, that voices or psychic impulses were making him do what he did. But could the psychiatrists reasonably expect a psychotic to tell the whole truth? He knew that what he was doing was objectively wrong, yet he could not resist: it was what he had to do to remedy crimes he'd committed in a previous life.

All day we tensely waited for the phone to ring. A psychiatrist called to say that they were re-examining his case. They would get second and third opinions. At the end of that day a final call came. They had changed their minds. He was being kept at the Clarke.

Over the next few days Alison rallied family and friends to testify that the way Malcolm had behaved of late was totally different from the way he had been before his breakdown. Meanwhile, he was transferred to another floor. A different psychiatric team was at work there. They didn't assume he was a consummate actor.

Dr. S. had changed, too. He was now abashed, conciliatory, and co-operative. As for Malcolm, he was quieter, though still given to pouring juice, soup, or sunflower seeds on himself while on outings. We enquired about other treatment options, if any could be found. Maybe a quiet, structured religious community might take him. Events had been so rough at the Clarke we couldn't help wondering if almost anything would be better.

*

AT SOME POINT Alison conducted what amounted to a long interview with Malcolm. She transcribed it. In broken part it read:

> *Why were you smiling at nothing in the two weeks from Fred's breakdown to your breakdown? Were you thinking about appalling things to do and smiling at the idea?*
>
> No, I was smiling at nothing so as to bug you, Mum. I wanted to worry you and mess with you. Because it is interesting.
>
> *There was a time when you were nine or so and you were bug, bug, bugging your dad and me until we exploded and yelled at you, and I even may have spanked you and I said, "You know that drives us nuts. Were you deliberately trying to make us mad?" and you said, "Yes." And I said "WHY?" and you said, "Because it's interesting." Is that sort of the same thing as now?*
>
> Yes, that's it exactly.

Exploring madness, the experience of being mad?
Yes.

Because it means I don't have to be adult. It's a way of getting away from responsibility.

I have had six weeks of no responsibility and it hasn't made me better. I need to start being given responsibilities — put me to work around the house.

When you are asked why you are doing something, and you answer, "To get attention," does that seem like the real reason, or a reason that you are inventing to explain something that you don't understand?

I feel that I am inventing it after the fact. There has to be some sort of explanation, so I make one up as best as I can.

You are NOT to explore badness anymore. You are to absolutely STOP. It is not to be tolerated, and we won't. You will be out of here, and you will be on your own and the decision will not be reversed. Do you understand?

When Fred said, "I am sorry I got you into this" what did he mean?

He gave me the idea of exploring what it was like to be mad.

When you said, "It's a combination of depression and exhibitionism" was that an after the fact explanation, or does it feel like the real explanation?

It's an after the fact explanation.

I feel as if I have two heads — and one of them is making these decisions, doing these things.

*

ONE SUNDAY HE began to weep, asking, "Am I going to be like this for the rest of my life?" I couldn't answer him. Another day he asked me thoughtfully if a cure would ever be found for schizophrenia. It was hard to imagine a vaccine like the ones used to cope with smallpox or polio. I said that I expected there would be. But I didn't know when.

He still tentatively tried to upturn cups of tea on his head when we went out for a snack. What was different now, and a great improvement, was the psychiatrists' attitude. Either because Alison and I had scared them, or because they got wise in some other way, they are now apologetic and no longer thought he was bad, not mad; his parents were no longer part of his problem; and the certified insanity of attempting to discharge him untreated to go to his choice of street shelters would never reoccur. He saw different psychiatrists, and took different tests. What a useless term *schizophrenia* was! It was a mere label of convenience. Not only was it made to embrace a fog of symptoms, subdivided into multiple categories, the medical profession was pharmacologically lunging in the dark in a duel with certain brain chemicals. And the chemicals had genetic origins.

*

COMPARED TO THE ACW, Malcolm was now in a quiet ward, a rectangle of rooms. A phone was in the hall. There was a laundry room, and people lunched in a room with a TV and couches. They were escorted out on excursions, took art therapy, played table tennis. Among them was Fred's brother Phil. With Fred in and out of hospital, balking at taking medication, the family's hard luck hadn't ceased. At meal time a few other patients, men and women, young or old or middle-aged, sat scattered at tables, waiting for a metal curtain to slide up and reveal the laden steam table and have lunch dished out. They were mostly silent, though one of them was talking rapidly to himself, and another one, in a black slouch hat and untidy overcoat, was loudly complaining about many unresolved grievances. They moved somnambulistically toward the dispensation of their penne in tomato sauce.

Since Alison had her job, I was the one to take Malcolm on his outpatient visits to CAMH. Out the back door to the lane then around the corner to Bathurst and Alcina. The Number 7 bus south to Bathurst subway station. One stop east to Spadina. Transfer to the Spadina streetcar, get off at College abreast of CAMH. Repeat. Once, transferring to a streetcar at the subway station, he abruptly declined to go further. I had to coax him onward, just as I had to sit with him in the ER waiting room after he had one of his episodes, which might involve the familiar bump-bump-bump of his descent down the stairs, or his trying to trash his possessions. I would juggle a phone to call a taxi, at the same time trying to keep him from doing further damage.

There was always something outlandish, silly, in my attempts to physically restrain him. As I held him, tried to keep him from taking off all his clothes in public or, on the worst occasions, wrestled with him on the floor, he would tickle me, as if it were a childhood game. I felt sorry for myself: what was a man in his sixties doing, doing this? Once I had to phone 9-1-1. By the time the police arrived, he had settled down. I'd read horror stories about how cops had mishandled out-of-control psychotics: with Malcolm they were gentle. I rode with him to the Clarke in the back of their car while he sat beside me handcuffed. They gratefully released him to the ER staff.

Sometimes it seemed to me that for what remained of time I would sit with him in the locked waiting room of an emergency ward of a psychiatric hospital while inside a glass-walled paddock the staff wandered on undisclosed errands among their whiteboards,

charts, and pigeonholes, or sat staring indifferently at their un-
informative computer screens while outside it the waiting room cli-
ents slumped in somnolence or in various states of uncomplaining
pissed-offedness while the seconds, minutes, and hours ticked by
and the television mounted above our heads silently reflected the
latticed lights of the ceiling and the outdoor joys of scenic Alaska.

At home, he mostly slept. The large, lulling doses of the antipsychotic drug risperidone were taking hold, though I supposed
he also must have been exhausted from the traumas his body had
been put through. It was living with a narcoleptic. He would sleep,
sometimes until noon, and then doze on the living room couch for
the rest of the day. That was it, apart from meals. Then it was time
to go to bed.

Gradually, he was able to apply for menial jobs at least. He last-
ed two months assisting at a veterinarian's, preparing animals' food,
taking them for walks, cleaning their cages. He lost that job: maybe
he'd been sleepwalking or just going through the motions.

Always on the lookout for a job in the caring professions, volunteer or otherwise, Malcolm saw a help-wanted ad on Charity
Village, an online clearing house for people who gave their time
to good causes. The ALS Society was seeking a volunteer visitor.
Malcolm applied and heard back from Louise, who was in charge of
visitors; she'd often worked at hospices for people dying of cancer,
AIDS, or ALS. At present, ALS patients were her specialty. ALS,
amyotrophic lateral sclerosis, often called Lou Gehrig's disease,
after the great baseball player who died of it, is an incurable disease
that affects nerve cells in the brain and spinal cord, causing loss of
muscle control. As the disease worsens, the nerve cells become damaged and the patient loses control of the muscles needed to move,
speak, eat, and breathe.

Serendipitously, Louise was the sister of Mitzi, a volatile
Irishwoman with whom I'd long had an enjoyably fractious

friendship. We did a lot of laughing together and, once in a while, had an alcohol-fueled brawl. Mitzi did the art design for *The Idler*, a journal of comment and the arts to which I contributed. She had forthright opinions and solid good taste. Malcolm fought shy of women like Mitzi he considered to be overly assertive. Notwithstanding, they became friends.

Louise, who ran the training program for volunteers, was cautious about hiring people; visiting ALS patients was a demanding job. Malcolm was understandably uneasy at first but, interviewing him, Louise soon concluded that he was "an old soul," wise beyond his years. He took copious notes and asked many questions — good signs. In his training they talked about communication and spirituality. Unlike many volunteers he knew how to listen, how to discover what was in a person's mind at the end of his life. Only 10–20 percent of volunteers worked out. He was frank and open about his psychosis. In fact, it was an asset from Louise's point of view that volunteers had struggles of their own. She never doubted for a moment Malcolm was the right person to visit the dying. She thought that, kind and sensitive, he was brave to take on the task. He never talked or wrote about his patient, but that was to be expected. Volunteers were pledged to extreme confidentiality.

Malcolm was assigned George, who was in Bridgepoint, a hospital a block north of the Broadview and Gerard mini-Chinatown on a crest overlooking the restless to and fro of traffic on the Don Valley Expressway. Bridgepoint combined the functions of rehab and palliative care, the optimistic and pessimistic, the positive and negative. Bridgepoint was only a few blocks from a little vegan restaurant called Simon's Wok. At Simon's Wok he befriended a young Chinese man about his own age who was a Taoist priest, as Malcolm told me with some pride. The Taoist priest apparently had divinatory powers. After examining Malcolm's hand, or whatever he examined, he told him he should not make any long-range plans.

Malcolm had been getting regular visits from what CAMH called a HIP team, which had nothing to do with orthopedic surgery or being trendy. They would ask how depressed he was on a scale of one to ten. Part of the HIP team's job was to gauge what side effects the antipsychotics were having. The answer: eye spasms, muscular stiffness. He was still sleeping too much, mainly a side effect of the risperidone. He was also taking more-or-less-experimental Prozac, prescribed because he seemed to be mildly depressed. Who wouldn't be, under the circumstances?

Was he taking the right pills? Were they compatible with each other or did they conflict? With a murky disease like schizophrenia even the right prescription might be the wrong dosage. We lived in fear of forgetting to give him pills. At the same time I had little faith in them.

I briefed Bill on Malcolm's progress. It was possible to say there was progress. Generally, he was cheerful, easy to live with, and obliging about doing chores. And he was coping well with his two courses — he'd got a 90 for a journal-entry assignment in the Aboriginal Religion course. (On his own, he was also taking an extracurricular yoga/meditation course one night a week, though he was meditating much less than he used to pre-breakdown.)

He now had a new psychiatrist-and-nurse team, a sign of progress, since the former team specialized in the first, most dangerous, phase of recovery from psychosis. However, he scared the shit out of me when he revealed to Alison that he occasionally smoked dope. We talked and talked to him about the dangers of street drugs; it was also disturbing that, despite being repeatedly asked by his psychiatrist and nurse during that period, he'd denied having taken a toke. They were now informed. Whereupon some idiot or idiots gave him another toke. On his way to class he had a panic attack. When he told me about this, I spent an hour or so berating him and he promised not to smoke dope again. He didn't really consider pot as a street drug in the same league as LSD, speed, ecstasy, etc. I told him there was no quality control in pot and he could never know whether or not it was spiked with something else.

One trouble was that he had a very small circle of friends, including of course Fred, the schizophrenic who'd carved himself up a week prior to Malcolm's own breakdown. Fred was of little help. He had decided to stop taking his meds.

Malcolm was as much interested in spirituality and otherworldly matters as before, though this hadn't caused his breakdown but merely furnished the content of it. (If he had been Jewish, the content would have concerned the Talmud, rabbis, etc., just as the psychosis of Fred, who was scientifically inclined, focused on science and numbers.)

By email, Bill quizzed him with probing questions. Malcolm said he would "try to put as much thought into answering them as you did in posing them." With the New Year approaching, Bill asked Malcolm about his goals, and whether he was content with his life. The reply:

> In a sense yes, I am happy. It's been a long time since i was able to say this with confidence but i can now. I am surrounded by love from my friends and my family and love for my self.… In another sense, i have alot left to do and though i have learned much already there is still more i wish to know and my task at this time is to figure out how i am best able to serve.

What did he intend to do about it, Bill asked. "Well, find a girlfriend for one thing. Make some new friends, expand my social circle, things like that." He planned on taking a course in comparative mysticism, a course looking at how cultures can harmoniously interact, and a course relating to the connection between spirituality and environmental studies. None of which his lawyer uncle would have approved of especially. About work the next summer he planned on working security again, which had "a flexibility that allows me to plan outings with friends." He admitted that he needed "to contribute toward his education. Its time to push myself a little bit (or a lotta bit) because i have been recovering for a year and its time to get back in the work force."

What would he do when he finished university?

1. Teach english in another country. There i can experience another culture and make money to support myself. It will also give me time to think of what i want to do next.

2. Learn a marketable skill. I would like to do something hands on. Massage therapy is one idea because i can help people, learn about physical well-being, and give really good massages.

Continuing in guidance counsellor mode, Bill asked him to itemize his strengths and weaknesses.

Weaknesses:
Sometimes i have difficulty focusing on a task for a long period of time.
Sometimes i have trouble getting started at things.
Sometimes i think abstractly or philosophically when a more practical approach is needed.
I don't think i feel emotions as strongly as other people.
Sometimes i let my imagination carry me away with it.
Sometimes i am too shy.
Sometimes i procrastinate.

I am not self sufficient
I have difficulty making new friends

Strengths:
I can grasp some difficult philosophical concepts
I am a compassionate person
I keep a good relationship with many old friends
I am a creative person
I am fairly attractive physically
I am open minded
I have a good education
I am funny
I have a great deal of love for those dear to me
I listen to my elders

Was he happy living at home?

Yes, very.

That was reassuring.

Years ago, at Alison's request or on my own initiative, I had taken on the task of composing a letter to Santa Claus on his annual visit, accompanied by a small gift: cookies and perhaps an apple for Rudolph. Malcolm took over the task. For himself he requested Nicorette gum to curb the smoking he had regretfully taken up, lip balm, and some AA rechargeable batteries so he could run his Walkman. Chocolate was always good: chocolate-covered cherries, rum-filled chocolates, Big Turks, Caramilk bars. Crystal or semi-precious stones that he could use in his jewelry-making, anything glow-in-the-dark, including beads, bracelets, and stars. Art supplies, especially mechanical pencils and erasers, Pilot fineliners.

He had resumed working for a security firm that paid minimum wage and docked him for the cost of a uniform. He liked it. He would be stationed late nights in a deluxe department store or take part in crowd control at a rock concert or soccer game. What security duty offered was lack of stress. Stress was a psychotic trigger.

What could amount to stress was unpredictable. A busboy job at the Golden Grill did it, though. One day he dumped a cup of yoghurt on his head and was prompted to shout out on the subway on the way home. Stress never seemed to arise from the stresses and strains of domestic life, or from any row Alison and I might have, or from what he might have sensed of my own problems and anxieties, financial, medical, or professional. The biggest test came when Alison revealed she'd been oppressed by suicidal thoughts for some months. She could imagine no good future for any of us and considered it would be a kindness to end our lives. Malcolm would end up as one of those lost mad mutterers who gibbered to themselves on city buses. She would kill herself and take Malcolm and me with her. I listened calmly, but inwardly I was enraged she would have the unspeakable arrogance to decide our fate. One could soppily suppose she was doing it out of misdirected love for us. But could she be trusted to safely drive a car with us in it down a hurtling highway?

Malcolm was no longer going to the Clarke but to the Queen Street West branch of CAMH: "999 Queen" had long been a Toronto synonym for psychiatric hospital. I took Alison along to his next appointment there. She told the psychiatrist about what she'd been feeling. He took her seriously. We took a taxi to the Clarke, where she spent overnight, parked on a cot. The next day she was shifted to the locked psychiatric ward at Mount Sinai, the same hospital where we had taken Malcolm at the onset of his own crisis. During her confinement there her palms sweated and her blood pressure shot up from panic attacks, her treatment complicated by the fact she was invariably much more intelligent than most of the professionals who were treating her. They allowed her home on overnight passes before her final release.

Through all of this, Malcolm remained perfectly calm.

*

ONE STAR OF the recovery program was Marie, an assertive, pretty Filipina (or possibly Spanish, since grandparents on both sides of her family were Spanish) with raven hair. She was about Malcolm's age, and with the same weight gain he had. She had undergone her first episode much earlier than he had — untypically, because the usual window for the onset of psychosis was from the mid-teens to mid-twenties for males, but for females some years older. A university graduate, she taught English as a Second Language.

She and Malcolm had instant rapport, and it wasn't long before she was spending overnight at our place. What happened in bed between them I didn't know, and didn't want to know, but it was wonderful he had found someone, his first dating partner in years. He met her attractive family — parents, sister, and brother — and could often be reached at their home. A devout Catholic, she took him to Sunday mass at St. Michael's Cathedral. Conversion to Roman Catholicism didn't seem immanent, though. He divided his nights between our house and her parents' home, which sometimes led to confusion and cross purposes. Where was he tonight?

Alison yearned for a kitten to join the two cats we already had. Like her, Malcolm could never have too many cats around. She found one offered for sale on a classified-ad website. She and Malcolm went to fetch him. The cost: $5. After the usual discussion about names I called him — over Malcolm's objections — Rastus.

A racist name, but I liked the sound of it, and its associations with "raffish" and "irascible." He had a small head on a big body, and what I called "a criminal face." He specialized in mugging Barnaby, and grew hugely, becoming an adult cat in size but a frenetic kitten in mentality. Malcolm liked to watch him attacking a cushion.

An inveterate teaser of animals, I hoped to inspire jealousy by stroking one cat in the presence of another, saying, "Rastus is a *good* cat, Barnaby is a *bad* cat." Or vice versa. Malcolm detested my doing this. It *was* a bit bizarre, I realized. He got the notion that there was something unhealthy about my relations with the cats. One evening, he was lying on one couch, I on another. He was watching something on TV; I was doing nothing. Barnaby jumped into on my lap. Malcolm glared at us, clenching and unclenching his fists. "Are you OK?" I asked.

"I'm fine," he said.

I said, "You're glaring at us." "Glaring at *us*?" he said.

"All right," I said. "Glaring at me."

The kitten lay on its back while I stroked his belly. Again the glare. This time he accused me of sexually molesting it. Bestiality had never been one of my vices. Angry, indignant, I found this a new variation of craziness. At some level Malcolm understood this. Out in the hall he said tearfully to Alison, "Why am I such a jerk?"

*

THOUGH WE HAD to constantly remind him about medical appointments, over time he became an exploitable success story to the part of CAMH that served recovering, or at least coping, psychotics. LEARN was located west a long streetcar ride away: offices and meeting rooms large and small; a coffee-maker, microwave-equipped kitchen; patients' artworks on the walls. The hub for get-togethers. He quickly made friends; our main contact was Sabrina, a cheerful, obliging former Rhodesian and a family worker in CAMH's First Episode Psychosis Program.

About a year after Malcolm had been admitted to CAMH we outlined for Sabrina all that had had gone wrong during his treatment. Of course, we could also have written a much longer memo about what went *right*, for example, the sympathetic treatment he got from nurses in the Acute Care Ward; the care and attention he got from psychiatrists and staff on the tenth floor ward, and during home visits he'd received since he was discharged. We tried to be as neutrally objective and factual as possible in chronicling what Malcolm had undergone at CAMH, how Dr. S. had accused us of being "litigious." We had also resented it when he said Malcolm could be charged with sexual assault involving a Black nurse, and when he said that it was all right to be "mad" but not "bad." Nor was it helpful when the Clarke social worker who had been assigned to Malcolm from the beginning provided us with a list of $200-an-hour career counsellors.

Malcolm was enlisted with other psych-ward alumni to star in an informational inspirational video called *Beyond Psychosis*. In it, each of the leading lights was to make a short positive statement. His was "You are stronger than you think." When his turn came he had trouble making out the cue card, having forgotten his reading glasses. What he said was, "You are *stranger* than you think."

*

NOVEMBER 10, 2008, 6:00 p.m., the University of Toronto Fall Convocation, Honours Bachelor of Arts. A day we thought would never come. Untidy gowned lines formed upstairs at Trinity College. With Marie, we took balcony seats. Convocation Hall had become a terraced amphitheatre of roosting magpies in black and white. Row after row of the tiered students descended to be pronounced graduates, shaking hands with dignitaries and the chatty chancellor. Mothers and fathers, sisters and brothers, boyfriends and girlfriends sat eager and restless, edged to the balcony rails to click pictures, now and then uttering war whoops. One young man climbed the podium to get his diploma. From a far corner came a shout from a parent: "You're on your own now!" Then it was Malcolm's turn. My God, he had graduated!

After, we went to the Queen of Sheba, an Ethiopian restaurant, to celebrate. During it, though, Marie had one of her meltdowns, quietly weeping. This would happen now and then. She would be her usual buoyant self, and then dissolve inwardly and collapse. I wondered what kind of future she and Malcolm could have, given the weight of problems they both had to overcome. Like Malcolm, she was taking an antipsychotic pill, to which was added an antianxiety and an antidepressant, so God knew what side effects this cocktail created. She plainly wanted to be in love, and it seemed Malcolm did, too. I would see them walking up the street hand in hand. But she phoned him up to eight times a day, each call amplifying the one before. She was physical, emotional, tactile in a way that, taking a cue from his father, Malcolm wasn't. He said he began to feel smothered, and she was aware of that, at the same time compelled to make him respond to her needs. They went to the brink of breaking up several times, each time retreating, and she would call on me for counsel. I could calm the churning waters temporarily. I couldn't help noticing how extraordinarily articulate she was. She could itemize points as deftly as a psychotherapist, and probably knew more about psychotherapy than they did. When Malcolm felt incompatible with his psychiatrist she brought matters to a head for good or ill, vigorously advocating for him when he went along for what turned out to be a showdown. The result was that Malcolm ended his sessions, which in turn led to a search for a new psychiatrist. Meanwhile, their own relationship continued to be fraught. Alison had always sought to encourage it, and to assure Marie she was on her side. She thought they should relax, and let love happen.

That was not a prospect. They parted, resolving to be good friends. I didn't place much stock in the good intentions. To my mind, romance was unlikely to phase into friendship, at least as I understood it. The phone calls grew further and further apart.

*

THE DAY AFTER his graduation I went with Malcolm and Marie to see that fifteen-minute video, *Beyond Psychosis: Exceeding Expectations from First Episode to Recovery*, in which Malcolm starred, screened in the *Rendezvous with Madness* film festival held at CAMH's Queen Street location. "Sharing facts and personal stories, 5 young people talk about their experiences with psychosis and recovery. As they confront the myths and stereotypes surrounding mental illness each one of them offers a sense of hope and inspiration to people living with these issues." I wondered what would become of them all.

*

ALISON THOUGHT RASTUS and Barnaby ought to be indoor *and* outdoor cats; Becky had long been one. Alison put a phone number tag on Rastus's collar. I'd grown fond of him. He might have been a mongrel, but he had a personality. Late one warm afternoon I was communing with him in the living room. He licked my nose. He wanted out. He did not return that night. In the morning a stranger phoned me. She had got our number from the collar of a cat she'd found. He was dead.

Pulling on gloves, I took an old towel and crossed the street. I found him at the curb, stiff, his mouth half open. A car must have hit him. I wrapped him in the towel and took him to our basement, putting him in an empty file carton. I phoned Alison. She wanted to come home but her boss said she couldn't.

When Malcolm got home I told him what had happened. He went to the basement to be alone with what was left of Rastus. Afterward, we dug a grave at the side of the backyard and put him in it, covered him up. If you counted Malcolm's expired mice, and other casualties buried there over the years, our backyard could qualify as a pet cemetery.

Malcolm missed his personality and presence. But it just felt like he had gone missing, not like he was gone forever.

*

AT THE BEGINNING of October he wrote:

> The search continues for a girl-friend. A female companion of some kind. I would like her to be an old soul like me, a good friend from the past remembered through the fog of incarnation. I want someone to fall in love with. A person who is like me, who I am sexually compatible with, who likes to dance, who is spiritual, who is loyal to me, who has a sense of play. She doesn't have to be beautiful, I'd almost prefer her not to be. I just want her to be cute, and cuddly. I hope I meet her soon, I'm almost ready — I think.
>
> I had a series of lucid dreams the other night. I called for my guides but they never came. I am learning the value of patience. I think my old guides have

returned. We'll I'm not sure but it feels comfortable to believe in them again. I like them a lot.

The next day he wanted

to know whether my old guides have returned or whether I am imagining them. I can see their faces clearly in my mind but then again I can create anything in there so I just can't know. I saw them once, they appeared to me out of thin air and I saw their faces and I knew. Since then I had been talking to them but I don't know how much was actual conversation with them and how much was me just talking to myself. I still felt that they were in the back somewhere guiding my thoughts even if they weren't talking directly. I often put words into their mouths but I wonder how much that was me actually hearing them and echoing it in my own mind. Am I not meant to know for certain? Will it aid my spiritual growth to have to wonder and question. Does it make me stronger to tie my beliefs in knots and then find a way through. Is the truth that much more refreshing when we return to it after being away so long. I wonder why not just be blatantly obvious about their existence. Perhaps their visits are meant for special occasions. I'd like them to be my 'everyday guides' like they used to be.

In a few days he was pleased to say

Things are really progressing. Things are changing so fast that I am reluctant to write things down. It seems like as soon as I am certain about one thing it changes the next moment so the best way to deal with my spiritual friends is to remain in a state of flexible uncertainty. Whether I am talking to them, to myself, or a combination I am learning a great deal about myself and new ways to thing and feel. It's interesting that I don't receive knowledge so much as wisdom. I don't receive new information so much as I receive new ways to process it....

So what do I write about?

I would like this to be a magical journey. I would like to write things here that I am not able to put into my written journal. Stuff about my meditation exercises, my spirit guides, my rituals, my telepathy and energy play. Perhaps I should start from the most recent and work back. Today I meditated lightly, I didn't go too deep, on top of about 5 or 6 cups of warm sweetened coffee. I don't think I made contact with them. My guide just said I did. Well maybe I should write it that I am always sort of in communication with them, that is their presence is always influencing my thoughts. When they are around me its like my thoughts get deeper, they say that when I connect with them the information flows in that is beyond words. I like to think of it as liquid communication where meaning is melted. The number of guides is not important at this point but simply to understand the information that flows in. Listen for their vibration and allow it to pass uninhibited deep into my consciousness. What I am writing is the surface consciousness and the information has to bubble up for it to be perceived. In time, they say, my thoughts will become more liquid and I will understand them more readily.

They say that for communication to occur I have to get the ball rolling, it is an interesting challenge to keep my own thoughts and feelings running parallel and not let one or the other overwhelm. It is a nice feeling, like drawing with someone on the same page. It is I that must push forward, actually Us that must push forward, concentrate, think new thoughts and learn. We learn by creating, we learn about ourselves and our relationship to our Source who is the beginning and the end. The seed of ultimate compassion, consciousness, unity exists within us. It is the flame of pure personality flavoured by the lessons we learn and the experiences we have on our journey home. As we go on we shed the layers of self as we grow and expand as spiritual entities becoming more fluidic as we enter higher frequencies of consciousness ...

He enrolled in an astral projection class.

I am going to study and work towards the goal of leaving my physical body while being full conscious. I have tried before, a couple of times almost succeeding before my heart started racing and pulled me back in. I also had the feeling of drifting out then being lowered back.

However, he wrote, he would like to talk of other topics, especially his

frustration with communication. It just feels like I never get anything new, it is all just stuff which I already know or could have made up myself. Sometimes it doesn't feel as if I get anything truly original. I don't mean to insult my guides and perhaps it is simply the lack of awareness on my part. Perhaps if I had spent as much time practicing as complaining I would know by now. The word is patience, and I am learning. But is it my impatience that tells me that there is a major threshold I must reach to progress, some kind of barrier I must pass. Perhaps it is simply my own fear. Perhaps it is the echoing shield with which I surround myself. I can't believe that the whole thing was my creation. It is too good, I've learned too much. I love to chat with them and yet one of my greatest fears is falling back into insanity, of losing my grip, of getting lost in myself and not hearing the True Voices anymore. Though I know that to be an impossibility, yet I'm afraid. Somehow I know I have passed some sort of test. I did what I believed was right, it felt right to do it. A big question I want answered is was it me who was testing myself or someone else as well. Was it simply a malfunction of the brain? Was it providence?

It feels like I am only given a little bit to guide my curiosity, I am only given a little bit to keep me hungry, if feels like I am being teased, played with, flirted with but no commitment from anything. Is this the best environment for my growth? When will the real teaching begin. I know I am being taught now, but when will I pass the threshold. A better question is why do I think I need a threshold. Am I not content now? No. I'm not content, I want to settle into a nice routine I want to come home but every time I look at my guides, every time I look at myself, I see a stranger looking back. Just when life was starting to get good, just when I was starting to tap into new worlds to explore and see things with new "I"s and learn to love I began to slip. If only I had kept my balance what would I have been today? I am too creative for my own good. I dreamt up such a tale, magical, epic, tragic, and wrong. So very wrong.

So why can't I let it go?

Is it the fire which fuels my searching? It is that little pebble in my shoe that keeps be aware of every step I take. The question by which I judge everything else, the shadow keeping me from seeing the light of the sun. I beg for that shadow to be lifted. I can't learn without fear, without pain can I?

He was soon thinking that it was

Time to take a break, take a breath and relax. I think this will be my last entry before I invite others to read it. I've written much of my journey, my quest for balance, my dreams, my friends. It has taken a decidedly magical twist that I am not all together comfortable with. Perhaps that is for the best ... Or is it? When I have made most of my discoveries I have been in a state of peaceful excitement but not this unrest. Is someone trying to tell me something. I am not referring to my online journal, what is here is for my eyes alone so I don't have to worry. But what of what is out there.

I am now faced [with] a major choice.

One, keep this journal to myself, keep it only for my eyes to see. Post this entry and forget about it. Leave it floating in cyberspace to be discovered by whomever comes across it. End it and continue privately.

Or two, invite close friends to read it. This is by far the more risky of the positions. But why, what do I have to lose? The respect of my friends? Is that likely? I've written truthfully, I think it's interesting stuff (a bit odd mind you, but that's nothing new to me). Have I been too open about my searchings, my path, should I obey the first rule of the magician: remain silent? I have placed this journal on the internet, a connected and diverse and incredibly open environment. But why? What do I hope to accomplish by doing so? I must examine my motives carefully....

He wrote of his "magickal progress." In the beginning, he wrote, he experienced

a kind of paralysis, it seems like there is nothing I should say ... I have to listen to this feeling but at the same time I feel an urge to create a beautiful collection of thoughts, experiences, and experiments that I can look back upon in years to come. Most magickal sources I have read encourage journal writing and so I do not think there is anything inherently wrong in doing so (but maybe I am an exception).

So what is holding me back. Fear perhaps, perhaps I am afraid of losing the sanctity of the experience. I pray that I find a way to create a journal that pays respect to what cannot be written, that demonstrates what can, and can serve as a reference for me to look back upon in years to come.

"Love is the Law."

Essentially, he was talking to himself, trying to sort things out. Solipsistic as it might seem, it was a great improvement over being controlled by demonic forces. By November he was ready, or at least willing, to sum up himself, mind, body, and soul:

Negative:
I'm too flabby
People can't relate to me and I to them
I will always be different and cut off from others
I am lazy
I'll never be normal
I am insane
Nobody really loves me
I am incapable of love, at least the way others love
I freak people out
I have trouble making new friends

Positive:
I am quite intelligent
I am unique
I am an advanced spiritual being
I am creative
I am dead sexy
I'm a good dancer
I am open-minded and experimental
I am a good compassionate person
I have made much progress and there is still much to learn
I am cute
I have lots of friends
I have good teachers
I am a good student

Neutral:
I am an abstract thinker
I exist between worlds
I have red hair
I am a wizard
I am magickal
I do not always know what the truth is

Perhaps not, and there was that overpoweringly negative "I am insane." Yet surely the tally was comparable to many that could be compiled by anyone his age.

Within a month he had a more frenzied than usual psychotic episode. I had to call the police, who took him to the Clarke — but not for long. He was back home the same night. Since his blood test was clean, the best guess was he'd inadvertently skipped a dose of medication. He was well enough, or chemically stilled enough, to fly to Halifax for a somnolent weekend with Bill, mostly watching TV movies.

Meanwhile, Alison and I had been recruited to take part in a "Family Training Workshop" entitled "Why Are Families Not Believed?" Good question. In organizing it, Sabrina, the family worker in the First Episode Psychosis Program, declared that families can be allies, not obstacles, in treating psychosis.

Meeting, we came from urban and rural areas, and from every corner of Ontario: the Greater Toronto area, Peterborough, North Bay, Kapuskasing, Temiskaming, Sault Ste. Marie, Thunder Bay … Most were women: social workers, or volunteers working in a health centre dealing with victims of trauma and violence, or in a community centre for young people.

We sat in a big circle. Alison told about the violent onset of Malcolm's psychosis. How he got better treatment after the initial misdiagnosis and was able to take university courses, hold part-time jobs, willingly swallow antipsychotic pills, join LEARN programs. When my turn came, I said that families should be treated the same way as anyone else under our system of law. They should be presumed innocent unless proven otherwise. To experience a son, daughter, brother, or sister go crazy was to some extent to go crazy oneself.

Psychoses typically affect people in early adulthood so that the son or daughter seemingly reverts to being a child. This itself creates turmoil, or the hugely depressing sense that the natural order of things has been reversed. But we could look at it another way, I said. In "normal" life, children can grow up to be physically and emotionally distant. They lead their own lives and, though their parents may be happy at their successes, or unhappy at their failures, they become separate units, perhaps starting their own families. The bonds we once had with our children weaken, sometimes even snap. But to see a child become psychotic is to renew what we once had, to remind us of what we continue to share. It brings us back to basics.

The first disturbing thing a family learns is that psychiatry is an imprecise science. It's a natural human instinct to seek causes, reasons, for a traumatic event. Labels like "psychotic," "bipolar," or "schizophrenic" are not explanations. Families have to deal with the fact the person they have known for many years has apparently, inexplicably, become someone else.

At once, the family of the affected person begins to think in terms of cause and cure. But caregivers quickly steer them away from such concepts. Psychoses, families learn, are a matter of brain chemicals somehow going astray. But cloudy predispositions and triggers may be involved: genetics, street drugs, stress. So much for cause. As for cure, they learn that certain antipsychotic drugs will, or may, have beneficial effects. But cure?

Craziness drives families crazy. My wife, I said — Alison was sitting beside me — sometimes had outbreaks in the chief psychiatrist's office and got little sympathy. I felt like physically wounding myself. I didn't yield to the urge, I knew how insane it was, but that didn't make it any less terrifying. Was this a form of solidarity with my son?

My main conflict with Alison, I said, was temporary. It was about the frequency of our visits to him. My wife wanted to see him every day; I preferred twice a week. She needed the contact; I needed a little distance. This might point out something about men, fathers, relevant to a son's or daughter's first-episode psychosis. Men tend to believe they have to be a source of strength when everything and everyone seems to be cracking up around them. The downside of this is they could seem withdrawn and unfeeling.

When social workers tell families that in the aftermath of an extended psychotic episode they should "lead their own lives," they mean that families should not become martyrs or slaves. Alison hated that phrase, I said, because it was manifestly untrue. The reality remains that a family's freedom is going to be curbed. To see a child become psychotic is to renew what we once had, to remind us of what we continue to share.

I had nothing more to say.

*

MALCOLM WAS EXPERIMENTING with sending energy to various parts of his body. During his peaceful night security shifts, he wrote, he had enjoyed sensing the energy within his body. He opened from the top and pulled energy down through his crown and third eye into his neck. Then he gently tugged at the area mentally and felt a shift and a large block dislodged itself, moving down to rest in his upper chest. He could not move it any lower although he wanted to flush it down. It wouldn't budge, so he sent energy to it and willed it to dissolve. He then flushed energy around the rest of his body and left it at that. Meanwhile, his friend Fred was on a rockier road to recovery. He went round to Ashley's home and, for no reason anyone could guess, smashed the rear-view mirrors of cars parked on the street.

Malcolm dispatched his current view of reality to his skeptical uncle in Halifax.

> It is important to bring the will into harmony with others and with the cosmos as a whole. We are stronger together than divided, and so the best way to bring our dreams into reality is to see every action we take as having an effect on (and being as result of) everything else. What truly serves the collective is what is best for the self and is the most effective means to bring about change in keeping with our unique version of what it means to be happy.

*

ABOUT THIS TIME Malcolm was enquiring of himself whether he might be gay. After talking about it for most of a week he told me one evening he was going to a gay bar. I didn't combat the idea and in the event he couldn't contact the guy he was to go with. The topic fell away.

By mid-August there were other concerns. He crashed to the bottom of the stairs, punched himself in the head, followed by what was by then a familiar sequence: police, paramedics, an ambulance to the Clarke, interviews, an overnight stay on the tenth-floor ward.

By late August, though, he was well enough to go with Alison to a rented cottage at Go Home Bay.

*

CONSIDERING THAT I was a dedicated omnivore, and Malcolm had been a convinced vegetarian for some years, it was odd that we'd never had a fully developed argument about it. But eventually we got around to debating whether lobsters suffered when they were cooked; indeed, whether animals should be killed for food. I told him that as a farm boy I saw men wrap chains around the legs of pigs then, to the tune of horrible squealing, hoisted the pigs upside down and cut their throats. It was done that way so surplus blood could drain from the meat, and the blood could be collected for use as food. The pig could have been shot in the head, as steers were, but, given how hard it would have been to keep it still, somebody, not the pig, would have ended up shot. Even at that age I thought that our form of pig slaughter was a terribly barbaric way to kill an animal. I was anyway a very tender-hearted little kid and didn't go fishing because I empathized with what a trout felt when it had a hook in its mouth.

Later on I cooked lobsters. When I plunged a lobster headfirst into boiling water it took only a few seconds for it to stop moving. I told Malcolm that I didn't think that lobsters suffer in the way we mean when we use the word. Yes, as Malcolm rebutted, lobsters do have nerves. I said the lobster was a close relative to another crustacean, the sowbug. Our physiologies were very different. When a lobster loses a claw fighting another lobster on the ocean floor, as it sometimes does, does it feel "pain" as we would do on losing a limb? I didn't think so. Needless to say, our debate was inconclusive.

*

SOME MONTHS WERE uneventful. Malcolm was taking his pills. But in early December, after a day's busboy shift at Sunset Grill, he again dumped yogourt on his head and yelled in the subway.

A few days later, becoming rational, he was humorously writing Uncle Bill:

> Enclosed you will find (or have found) a 12-inch-long lock of hair, approximately 1/2 inch in diameter. Hold the hair in the light and you can observe that it is a reddish brown colour.
>
> Some explanation may be required.
>
> Buddhist sutras (religio-philosophical doctrines on the nature of the universe (dharma) and the unformed nature from which form arises (nirvana) as well the existance or non existance of the self) write that the nature of the cosmos is change. On December 7, 2006, I applied this principle to my hair. What you see before you is the result.
>
> I have mixed feelings about what has occurred but on the whole I think it is positive. The length of my hair represented a stage of growth in my life, and it is time that this growth is renewed. With the holiday season upon us and the new year quickly approaching it is time to take a moment (however long that may be) to reflect on what has occurred in the past year and make plans for the future. I hope this lock of hair will remain with you in a place of honour as a reminder of the importance of embracing change and welcoming the new.

Likely it was an agreeable task for him to itemize the Christmas presents he hoped to get. They included a warm hat and sweater, both without brand logos. Boxer shorts, New Age books. A subscription to a science magazine, semi-precious stones, interesting-looking beads or anything used in crafts and jewelry, pens and pencils for drawing, or other art supplies. He managed to ask what Bill wanted.

Toward the end of the month Aunt Rosemary, cousins Joe and Becca, and Becca's boyfriend arrived for a week's visit. On Christmas Eve, hell broke loose when we learned that, with Joe's help, Malcolm had bought some dope from his friend Nathan. Alison lashed out at Joe, who sullenly said, "What do you want me to do, commit suicide?" She snapped, "I wish you would." Rosemary was rightly furious: after all, during a troubled teenhood, Becca had — continuing a family tradition — attempted it.

*

THE NEW YEAR started. Malcolm's time was taken up with taking part in research studies like "Molecular Genetic Study of Schizophrenia" and churning out resumés for employment. He was taking his uncle Bill's advice to heart. He wrote:

> Another year has [*sic*] over and a new one just begun. What are my goals for another winter spring summer and fall that lies ahead of me.
>
> I am evolving and finding peace within myself. Perhaps I am becoming more mundane, it feels like my magical progress is at a standstill. Should I be meditating more? Playing deeper into my role: here, now, alive on this earth. What should be my next goal? Find a girl, settle down? Lose some weight, work out, grow stronger and healthier, be more enthusiastic. Embody the knight of swords.
>
> Seems like I have to work at finding things to say, finding new material. School starts tomorrow and with it comes work. I'll be starting a jewelry class soon as

well. Seems like everything's quieter now, I'm a man and so am one in a crowd. I don't think I stand out so much anymore, everyone I know seems at my level or higher. Perhaps it is time that I lose what keeps me apart from my friends and family. The sense of uniqueness that I once felt is fading. I am becoming normal.

Is this what it means to be a grownup, to have the flame of the new die to a glowing ember? Does everyone feel that everyone else has a center from which they draw inspiration and strength and that theirs is missing. I feel empty and I hope this is a positive sign. Lose my ego and allow my senses to be filled with the taste of life.

The New Year was not beginning promisingly for Alison. I got a phone call from Rosemary in Victoria. She said during the uproar around Christmas Eve Alison had threatened twice in front of Malcolm to kill him, herself, and me. I said that kind of hysterical outburst was very rare and that nothing like it had been said since then.

I talked to Alison about these suicidal urges and she disclosed the depth of her despair, which had been going on for a year and a half. Told about this, Malcolm's psychiatrist said Alison couldn't be his patient. But he referred her to the Clarke, which was where Malcolm and I took her. She was soon transferred to the psych ward at Mount Sinai Hospital. A week later she was home. Meanwhile, Malcolm had been quietly employed at Silver City cinema.

*

MALCOLM PURSUED HIS "Therapy Journal" in the New Year. At work he was feeling sluggish. His appetite increased and he gained weight. He felt more stable, though, and his thoughts seemed easier to manage. He wondered whether he'd get used to a new higher level of risperidone.

Mid-afternoon in late January I heard a crash. Malcolm had swept all the books off two shelves in his bedroom. At his own prompting he took a dose of risperidone.

*

ONE DAY HE came upstairs to my office and timidly told me that Alison was draining a bottle of vintage port that her father had bequeathed to her. It turned out she'd been drinking heavily for months, hiding the bottles. It wasn't the end of the excitement. I went out that night. Upon my return I found a note that she and Malcolm had gone to the Clarke Emergency. Malcolm, I learned from Marie, had eaten cat food, put toothpaste in his hair, and hit himself. He spent overnight at the Clarke.

*

MALCOLM HAD BROUGHT yet another notebook to kill time. His friend Benny once said, "Killing time is murder!" Now Malcolm wrote:

> Time is precious despite the fact that we have eternity
> to explore ourselves and learn new ways to experience
> our existence as conscious entities.
>
> So here we are, a small facet of a greater whole.
> Each moment contains part of eternity being one wish.
> Should I be somewhere else doing something else.
>
> Marie and I visited Fred yesterday which was his
> birthday. He's sedated due to his meds but you can tell
> he's still there beneath it.

I had seen a movie with him and Phil two days ago. Fred smelled like pot. I advised him against it but I myself experimented when I was first put on meds. Now I don't even drink alcohol or caffeine.

Though meds may dampen emotions and thoughts there is a part of me that can never be touched, never destroyed — deep within us, the spark of the Divine.

To move from the ego-personality to the True or Higher Self is a different journey for everyone. Some seem to have the trail blazed for them and they are clear from outward to inner selves. Maybe they have worked hard in past lives or they have chosen a direct path. Other souls, maze-like, struggle for lifetimes to find their way. Perhaps they like the challenge or prefer to wander on the journey home. I have tried to opt for the latter though longing for the former. I admire those who seem pure to the point of emptiness.

He kept having dreams about being on trial, a criminal. He missed Marie. He wanted to be there for her but maybe he couldn't. Alison's best friend Rasa, his sometime academic tutor, said it would only make things worse and cause her pain to stay friends. He hoped she was wrong. Ashley and he had stayed good friends. He was hoping the same would apply to Marie and himself. He missed her still, missed sleeping next to her and waking up beside her, the closeness.

We need to grow independently but it still hurts. Maybe that's a good thing. If we're too comfortable we do not make progress and I was comfortable with her. I can only hope I'm being prepared for something that God wants.

About Marie, he wrote,

> It hurts to know that I could help her or be the support
> she needs emotionally. I'm not sure I'm supposed to,
> that God intends it, I don't know how to love myself
> but I made progress with her. I loved the person I was
> when I was with her. Now we're both working and
> what good has come of that. I feel less myself and I
> don't know how to use the time that we're apart.

*

ONE WAY OR other, Hinduism was never far from his thoughts. It figured in the world religion courses he took at the University of Toronto, and in the reports he was assigned to compile after visits to temples, usually with other students. One temple visit involved meeting a person supposed to be an avatar of a female goddess who inhabited a male body. He went with his friend Adrian, who came to ask a blessing on his roller blades. He had forgotten them at home, however. To his regret Malcolm had not brought his crystal collection to be blessed as well.

The avatar seemed nice enough, but Malcolm could not overcome his Christian upbringing to worship her or even see her as a goddess. She, like the priests, was nude from the waist up and her male body smelled very much like a man.

Later he made another temple visit, this time with some classmates and their teacher. They greeted a priest there with the Sanskrit version of *namaste*, which meant "The light in me honours the light in you" or "the Divine in me bows to the Divine in you." It acknowledged that everyone was holy, longing for a relationship of unity with their creator. Perhaps that was why he always felt like he was coming home when entering a temple.

The priest who welcomed them said his mind could take him to India and back in a split second. Malcolm thought he meant he could remember India and the places he had been. He began to worry that this would turn into an inspirational speech about how, since we can imagine anything, we can do anything. He also worried that perhaps he was being too left-brained, too logical.

The priest said that the potential exists in all of us to make our dreams reality. Malcolm recalled the sleeping Brahma dreaming the universe upon his lotus. In a sense we were co-creators, but things were harder for us than for Brahma because we had to work to make our potentials manifest. "Life is not about drinking with buddies," the priest said, "It's about studying, being the best and rising to the top."

Malcolm thought that some of his most fulfilling times has been drinking with buddies (granted that he could not remember some of it) in that he grew and developed as a soul and learned more about himself, his friends, and what it meant to be alive. The moral Malcolm took from the priest was that only when we achieved peace with ourselves as limited beings, that is, only when we understood our limits, could we overcome them.

As in the Hindu festival of Holi, the temple was bursting with colour. Garlands festooned the walls glowing orange, green, yellow and gold, complementing the statues. The priest introduced the students to these figures. He lifted up the robes of Ganesh to reveal a small mouse statue at his feet. Ganesh, the elephant-headed god, was the god of business, patron of students, and the remover of obstacles. Elephants looked otherworldly to Malcolm. His head, he'd heard, represents the Absolute and his body the universe. He seemed wise and the curl of his trunk seemed, like the priest, mischievous and playful. There were other figures, too, and above them the creator figures of Vishnu and Lakshmi.

Images juxtaposed opposites, male and female, and might be balloons, candles, and flowers; there were lighted candles at the feet of the statues. They were called through a door to a statue in a corridor behind them that held devotional art in vivid colour, some hand-painted.

When it was time to go, someone brought in a big box of bananas and laid it before Vishnu and Lakshmi. The students got two bananas each to take home.

*

HE WROTE MARIE, thinking of it as a necessary act of reparation:

> This letter is my way of saying sorry for all the worry I've put you through. I love you and I hope that it will ease your mind and bring you peace insofar as that is possible.
>
> I want you to know that you will always be part of my life, a true friend and lover. I don't know the future but I do know that I will always seek you out for your wisdom, compassion and love. You have a remarkable way with words for healing, humour and guidance. I hope I have been the same for you.
>
> We have been many things to each other and loved each other in many ways both in this life and perhaps those that have past [sic]. We have always been close.
>
> Where do we go from here? Do we plan ahead or take each day as it comes? Do we turn inwards for advice or do we stay alert and present in our physical lives? We have much work to do in this world and I hope that much of the work we can do together. I think the best way to prepare for the future is to hold in the mind an idea, vision or feeling of what we want

life to be and then to surrender it to God. I want a
future with you in it, in whatever form is best.

This is a confusing time for us who are battling
psychosis. There are some periods I want to last forever. Time moves so fast. Be patient and know that I
will be there for you when you need me. If I seem uncertain about us know that it is not due to any fault on
our parts, it is instead part of the journey home which
is the ultimate goal. I wish I could make it easier for
us but an easy life is not always the best one. Please
keep me in your prayers as we find our way through
this labyrinth ...

"This is a confusing time for us who are battling psychosis," he
had written. That was for sure.

He added in handwriting: "Malcolm Sutherland." The signature was a personalized yet dignified touch.

*

IN THE EYES of his current CAMH overseers Malcolm was making
satisfactory progress. They enlisted him to talk to treatment neo-
phytes about his "recovery process."

I call it a process because it is ongoing. Healing is a
form of growth and I thank God that there have been
people able to help me and others recover.

If I could pinpoint a moment when my recovery began I would say that it was when I first actually told the doctors what I believed and let them
help me. Up till then I thought I was right and that
they couldn't understand. Believing that I could be

mistaken about my beliefs was a step that I had to take to get better.

In the hospital I slept, listened to music, made art and things began to get better. We found a medication that was effective and I was moved out of intensive care onto the tenth floor where I began to socialize and participate. Keeping busy was paramount and structured life on the tenth floor of the Clarke helped. My symptoms quieted down and with the help of family and friends I went out on passes and eventually was released. A month later I had my 21st birthday.

While I had residual symptoms I was able to work towards a full life, even returning to school for a semester. My energy was still low at this point but food tasted amazing and I put on weight. Again, lots of sleep and filling my time was key. It also took some discipline keeping my mind firmly in the present and what I was doing at each moment. Thinking back it was, and continues to be, a time that required patience both on the part of my caregivers and more difficult — to have patience in myself. I was slowed down but I had faith that I would come through it. It got better, my body adjusted to the medication, risperidone, and now the doctors have gradually reduced it. I now take 3.5 milligrams a day.

Since my release I have had about three or four "BLIPs" which stands for "brief limited intermittent psychosis" very short periods of about 15 minutes which go as quickly as they begin. These were triggered by lack of sleep, stress or use of street drugs. (I smoked marijuana once or twice which was a mistake.) I am now almost completely sober, I have given up pot and other drugs (aside from my meds) although I do drink alcohol from time to time.

If I was to offer advice to parents and caregivers I would say "be patient, they will get through this. Don't feel guilty, it's not your fault. Allow a generous amount of sleep."

If I was to offer advice to someone who has had the episode I would say "Be patient, you will get through this. Take your meds even if you feel completely healthy. And most importantly, don't do street drugs, even pot.

Echoing the counsel of his higher self, he said,

It just takes time, friendship, a healthy lifestyle and patience to become and stay completely healthy. Your growth will continue through the rest of your life and your days will get better and better.

Supplementing this optimistic prognosis, Malcolm wrote about his transition from first-episode psychosis to diagnosed schizophrenia. He wrote that he'd taken marijuana and alcohol at raves and dance parties. His symptoms, he wrote, began with paranoia, a feeling that other beings were communicating with him telepathically. He had long, elaborate conversations with God, Jesus, celebrities. What began as a manic internal dialogue soon turned darker and feelings of guilt arose because he believed he had been a bad person during past lives. Soon he was acting out on these feelings and believed he was being instructed to punish himself physically. He related how he'd given himself a black eye, how he'd slid down stairs, how he'd kept doing it for three months. How at the hospital he'd eaten his own shit. The care he'd been given, he wrote, "was for the most part extremely helpful with the exception of one doctor in the emergency ward." Fred, a close male friend of his, had had a breakdown a month before him. Instead of politely asking if they were in a relationship the doctor rudely commented, "Seems kind of gay ..."

Aiding his recovery, he said, were art therapy, friends visiting, exercise, plenty of sleep.

> Symptoms are vastly reduced but in times of stress they can emerge — just something I have to wrestle with — monitor my sleep, go easy on myself, I even go to clubs once in a while to dance but I never do street drugs though I do drink from time to time.
>
> On the whole my illness has made me stronger because I have kept my faith in God, love in my heart, and trusted that I would get through it. I have been challenged and I am overcoming the obstacles placed in my path.

He became confident enough to apply for a CAMH job as a "Peer Recovery Facilitator." Nothing came of it, though he had often been busy coping on the phone or in person with Marie's ups and downs. Her father's suggestions that she lose weight would put her into a tailspin, prone to an invasion of voices.

Like me, he was subject to fits of anxiety, panic attacks, though they were more severe than the ones that assailed me. When our Burmese cat, Barnaby, seemed sluggish, suggesting lily poisoning, he insisted I take him to a vet. A day later Barnaby was eating, peeing, walking around as usual the same as usual, but I was poorer by $226 for blood tests.

*

HE WROTE A candid letter to Tara, a trusted caseworker.

I've been experiencing symptoms again. It is difficult for me to put into words what I'm feeling. I wonder even if talking about things will make them better or whether it will just develop unwelcome feelings. I don't like discussing many of my beliefs from the beginning of my illness because I find that the more I discuss them the more instilled they become in my mind. So I'll choose my words carefully.

I feel like my illness is trying everything to convince me that I am a bad person. With depression, in my parent's case, the illness uses memories and current problems to bring about a state of angst or sadness in the person. Mental illness doesn't exist in a vacuum.

I worry a lot. When I am sick I worry that I was a terrible person in a past life, that I am unlovable, and that I am sick mentally, or even sexually ...

Beliefs that I am a bad person and the guilt accompanying them plague me. I am finding I am spending an equal time sick as healthy, if not more time sick. I am constantly fighting to believe that I am a good person yet I am weighed down. I have searched my memories of the past to see if there is anything that would warrant such extreme a feeling but there is nothing. I worry about this in that I might create false memories (I've heard this can occur in hypnosis).

My mind is often pulled into disturbing imagery but I resist this. I do not have urges to act on my beliefs like I did when I first got sick.

I try to have hope that this illness will be cured or at least managed. It is getting to the point where I

need more thorough help because I am sick of battling
with myself and struggling.

Yet he was able to go to the cottage at Go Home Bay that
summer with Alison and her brother Rob, and to keep his job at
William Ashley. Mind you, in late September he had a breakdown
on the job, a milder version of his early assaults on himself, and we
had to go to the Clarke, overfamiliar territory.

By mid-October he was so stressed out and overmedicated I had
to take him home after the funeral of Alison's Aunt Madeline rather than join the family wake. When her husband, Alison's Uncle
Jimmy, died Malcolm piously wrote,

> He joins Aunt Mad in heaven. I don't see it as an end,
> just a long vacation. I almost envy him in that he may
> rest and dwell in the Divine presence with his family.
> He is the last of a generation. He will be missed — at
> least until it is time for us to join him.

In small claims court I won a case against a deadbeat edi-
torial client. But this personal victory seemed empty when I got
home. It was depressing to learn that Malcolm had come back
from William Ashley's early, struggling to overcome his telepathic
voices. His problems could not leave me in enough peace to enjoy
good news.

In his journal, he signalled a big recovery.

> So it's over. My psychosis I mean — I'm sorry,
> present and past. Now is a time to move beyond
> healing myself and my own journey and start using
> what I have learned in the world around me.... Why
> am I here on earth, alive this day. To learn. To learn

about the way the universe operates and what is possible within it....

When a soul recognizes the voice of their Higher Self they awaken. At least that's how it was for me. Ascension is the process of perfection by which the individual, working with others, hears the Voice of their own source personality with God flowing through. This aligning with perfection is an ethical act since the perfect is the perfectly good.

*

MARIE HAD GIVEN him a hardcover therapy journal with unlined pages. In it he recorded that he'd gone to the career centre at the University of Toronto and registered on a job site. However, at the help desk he "felt weird." It was

like I was posing and everyone was watching. I often feel that way especially in public places. Sometimes I don't mind but I have to be careful what I say and think in case it is overheard.

Maybe it's a good thing. Being constantly observed. Maybe everyone is, if not by each other then by God. It is important to keep thoughts positive anyway to stay happy and successful and to make the music of the mind better. I grumble sometimes but that's clearing up too.

In late April he tabulated his moods. He was 70 percent "Discouraged." On the other hand, he was 60 percent "Happy" and 60 percent "Hopeful."

Discouraged	70%
Worried	40%
Sad	50%
Happy	60%
Hopeful	60%

He sought full- or part-time employment with an outfit called Grave-Side Funerals, promising to be "the kind of person who deals with the bereaved on your behalf in a sympathetic and respectful manner."

He didn't get the job.

IN THE THERAPY journal Marie had given him he wrote that he was "Sitting here at the kitchen table, waiting for the water to boil, in the quiet of the evening I think I may actually be happy. There is peace in this moment and I feel I can take a breath." He felt joy of a different kind when he went to a dance club where he had "an amazing time. I danced for about eight hours." Understandably, his legs were stiff the next day.

SUMMER HAD ARRIVED. With Goran's help he finished studying for a driver's licence exam. He was

> waiting and wondering what the next step is. I keep being pulled to be separate — at least, things work out that way. I missed Om but we had a party here at home.

I know God wants me set apart. I am pushed to create more peace and quiet in my life. I give up social activities to be by myself. I might fit in but it seems wrong to do so or even try.

So here I am. Waiting. Wondering what the next step is. Listening. Hoping one day to find others like me. What work do we have to do together. I know it will be my tribe calling. We all seem to spread out. Are we meant to congregate?

I know I am supposed to focus on God. But how do you focus on Him? Have does one pray night and day without repeating oneself?

A week later he was feeling

major feelings of disassociation. Seems like when I try to join the party I am going against God's will. Psychosis hits and I am on my own again. When I deliberately hold myself separate I am hated. Either way I am *separate* ... do I have to keep trying?

Loving yet separate. Perhaps unease/uncomfortable. Who do I trust? God, always but I wish he would make things clear. I have to share that balance. I miss people and if it wasn't for this illness I could share in what they have.

Lonely and exhausted from work. I was on my way to a mediation workshop and I felt intuitively like it was a mistake so I came home.

Spirit is still keeping me separate, I feel for some reason.

A few others are like me and we are all feeling the burden. Still, the moments of bliss and recollection and happiness are there and I have hope that there is a plan and we are all going to end up where we are meant to be. Ascension is a process and I wait.

Writing also helps, putting down thought and feelings. Reading also. How much though is psychosis and depression. I just follow where the spirit leads and I hope.

*

FEELING HOSTILE TOWARD Dr. G., his current psychiatrist — a hostility I didn't share because he'd been the doctor who'd rescued Alison when she threatened suicide — Malcolm left him, abetted by Marie, who also disliked him. In the doctor's stead, he wrote words of advice to himself.

Relax, it is just the illness. It will pass. You are getting better despite what you feel right now. People go through stages, you are going through one right now. Take this time to rest and focus. Connect with your higher self. Peace will come.

Advice sometimes came from that higher self. Perhaps it was a expression of the cognitive behavioural therapy that had become a common technique in treating mental illness.

Again, do not worry. Banish fear from your mind. Take it easy. Keep yourself busy. Focus on your connection to God and your higher self.

Be still and concentrate. I strongly encourage you to write, fill your time, work hard and follow what interests you If you have doubts be still and allow impressions to flow into your awareness. I have been watching and am pleased with your progress. Life is waiting. The time you have spent in peace and meditation is paying of [*sic*] and you are more confident and a clearer channel than you would be otherwise. Pick a path that feels open to you. Be unique and seek a new expression. There is an endless amount left to say. Be patient, learn and remember.

He sometimes added a stylized graphic signature to his higher self's recommendations.

His "Guardian Angel," who seemed to be his higher self's partner, had something to say, as well.

Hello old friend. It's been a while. You have been going through a lot of stresses and maybe that's a good thing. Life's challenges teach us about who we are and "what we're made of." I agree with your guides about not taking anything too seriously. You have a tendency to take a moment and make it into a rule. Let it go.

I do think that the best way to understand something is to look at it from a different perspective. Maybe that's what God is trying to teach you. Once you accept something, not necessarily agree with it but understand it you can move on. Trust yourself.

God is patient and will guide you but you need to trust. We love you and all of us in the higher dimensions wish you all the best during these troubling times. Reflect but do not ruminate. Focus on what you would like to see. Read books and keep up to date with the dreams of your friends. (Socialize.) Make time for yourself. You have been drifting. Look around you. Chat with me, I'm all ears. We've been together a long time and we look forward to working together in the future.

He began to ponder moving out to share a condo with a former schoolmate. Yet a voice cautioned,

Do not worry about living at home, accept it, there is no clash. Instead focus on gratitude for the home that has sheltered you for so many years (Are you so willing to leave?)

The Guardian Angel told him to cut down on eating dairy products, increase vegetable protein and fibre. He was advised

against starting any new romantic entanglements. You need to focus on yourself and your own progress before you can share intimately. We are preparing you — be patient.

His guides told him,

Be at peace. It is a belief in my circle that you are complete in each moment and that all your past (and future?) yes, are contained here and now. You are complete, Malcolm, we had to test you, understand you and now it is complete. Hear my voice and know that you are loved. Your time of trial is over. Be at peace.

At times the guides seemed to be penning horoscopes.

You have a wonderful and exciting time ahead of you. You will be meeting new people and learning new skills and more about yourself. All this interior work will have paid off.

He brooded about getting older.

I know people around me are settling down, even getting married. But I'm really not in that kind of headspace. I'm all for romance, even intimacy but I still need time on my own. I like where I'm at, being independent. I like the feeling of being able to hang out with who I want. I also like being alone. I'm all for dating and friendship but I'm not sure I want more than that. I also may still have feelings for a girl. I don't want to hurt someone by leading them on and not being able to follow through.

At the same time he was girding himself to deal with a new psychiatrist.

Malcolm, we can tell that the anticipation is growing. That is how it should be. We sense that you have made some progress. Do not be afraid of having passion provided it is in an expanded state. Love but cool that temper without growing cold. There is no problem with expressing affection but consider your self to be strong know your truth and, we say again, remain in your centre. Let things evolve and simply wait and rest. This is a time of preparation. Remain awake yet peaceful. Find quiet moments in your life. You may be feeling that remaining apart is easier, more

natural. Accept this, the paths are diverging. Focus
on our voice, we are always there, even when we are
quiet. There are those who will hang on just as you
have hung on. Love them but slowly release. There
will come a point where you may appear to be in the
same space but you know you are different. There will
not be as much friction as before partly because you
will know who you are and have accepted your destination. Do not resist simply dwell and be the most
honest and fullest representation of your essence in the
most loving expression that you can produce. You have
learned much and we have one final test of you: how
gracefully can you accept your destiny.

*

HIS NEW PSYCHIATRIST, Dr. D. was a young woman who, as she
got to know and like him, prescribed an antipsychotic medication,
Clozapine, to be phased in and risperidone, a.k.a. Risperdal, phased
out. For several years Malcolm had been on it at various dosage
levels. Its main variable side effect was weight gain and lethargy.
As well, it caused painful muscular spasms of his eyeballs, though
a drug called Benztropine corrected this. In early September Dr.
D. decided to be more "aggressive," since in her view Malcolm had
much potential for recovery. So many of her patients were no-hopers.
He wasn't. She explained that the main serious side effect could be a
sudden drop in the white blood cell count. She ordered weekly blood
tests. All through the fall his blood cell count was normal, and the
only side effect he reported was some drooling while he slept. He still
heard people cursing him wherever he went, worst in crowds and on
the subway. But he was more energetic and mentally alert. He was
even commissioned to tell other patients about his recovery.

He spoke to Marie on the phone and they agreed to keep their distance.

> We are both afraid of opening up old wounds. I like being independent but I know this will change later if I find the right girl.
>
> It makes it difficult to date when you feel it is wrong to go out at night. I think I need a change of scene — later anyway. Right now I seek the stability that home provides.

Three weeks later he wrote,

> Everything seems to be changing so fast it is hard to prepare … It is like I am being prepared for something. I wonder if it is one way I am being called apart or if that is psychosis.

When he went to the Royal Winter Fair with Alison — attending the fair each fall was one of her family's rituals — he

> felt out of place and uncomfortable in the crowd like I was being and these people thought I was a monster or worse. I almost believed them but I resisted that … is that right? It would be easy and in a way I do, to believe them and give in. But I struggle with that believing that it is my mental illness and besides — I'm always changing. Needless to say it was a tiring day.
>
> Maybe it is karma and I am dealing with material accumulated over lifetimes. I feel so paralyzed or like I have a constant psychic headache. I don't know what's

next. How can I be more ready than I am now. I fear
the worst.

He still missed his lost love Krista, the girl from the Ommie
weekend.

We sent some messages back and forth on Facebook
but nothing came of it. I wonder if she thinks about
me.

*

AFTER THE DEMISE of Rastus we were on the lookout for another
kitten. This time we decided to go upmarket, hoping to get a second
Burmese at a deep discount. After phoning a breeder in the exurban
town of Whitby, we found a possibility.

In a rented car the three of us one drove out there, taking a cat-
carrier along in case we found the right cat. In the breeder's brightly
lit basement we found a colony of beautiful creatures. One of them
was topaz-eyed and smoky-coloured. Certainly, he was not lacking
in the looks department. Three years old, he'd had a remarkable
career. He had been a grand champion at international cat shows,
sired kittens, some by his fellow residents — and, his service done,
had had his balls cut off. It seemed to be an ideal progress for a
male: glory, ecstasy, then philosophic calm.

The three of us conferred in the driveway. We decided to take
him. The breeder insisted that he must be an indoor cat. He had
never been outside in his life, except go to a summer cottage and to
cat shows. Besides, Burmese were notoriously prone to being cat-
napped. Malcolm felt bad limiting his freedom. On the one hand
Barnaby, now an outside cat, seemed the most contented he'd ever
been. On the other hand, Rastus had died after he was hit by a car.

Once we got him home, the new cat (now "Lancaster") and Becky ignored each other.

*

TOWARD THE END of November Malcolm was

> still having psychosis. I hear people calling me swear-words wherever I go. I do believe it is something or some way I am thinking that is causing it. Sometimes my thoughts but I'm sure it's that way with everyone. It's the worst in crowds and on the subway.

He was drawing schematic kabbalistic symbols, pentagrams, and angels, aware of friendly but spooky presences in the dark. He performed a "vibration of divine names," having memorized them beforehand. He felt a little guilty toward the end of the ritual about not involving God more. He resolved to say the next time a devotional prayer in Jesus's name.

He practised feeling comfortable in a crowd: creating peace around himself. He and Dr. D. chatted about medication and coping strategies. He told her his worries about thought-broadcasting. They were not going to increase the Clozapine as he had hoped — at least not yet, since it was a difficult medication to adjust.

He thought about Marie and how he missed the good times they had. She seemed like an all-or-nothing kind of girl. It was difficult to be friends with her if they were not in a relationship. They did communicate, after a fashion, on Facebook: "my dad's bday is coming up soon so i have to figure out what to get him. that's always a challenge."

He was sleeping eleven hours a day. When Alison and I went out to a party he wrote, "it feels a little odd to be here by myself. I used to love it but now it's different. I think if I moved out I would want to move out with people and not be in an apartment alone. Should I avoid going out?" He was still drawing pentagrams by candlelight, performing kabbalistic rituals, memorizing sacred names. He said them out loud when Alison and I were out but in a way it felt more natural whispering them. Meditating, he felt grounded and very in his body.

He did not neglect George, the ALS patient he was companioning, but he had to miss a day with him due to his H1N1 vaccine shot. He was being slowly phased off risperidone and onto Clozapine. He spoke to Marie on the phone but they no longer had much to say: being a couple had been such a huge part of their dynamic.

For my birthday he bought some deep-discount sweaters at Goodwill and overpriced single-malt Scotch at the LCBO. While he was doing his spiritual exercises, Lancaster complained at the bedroom door, wanting to come in. But Malcolm kept his door shut; he did not want a familiar. He found the air thick with energy, feeling it absorbed through his feet. He began study of the Lesser Banishing Ritual of the Hexagram (BRH).

A day later he had lunch and apple cider with Natasha at the Second Cup; she was "a wonderful person and a great artist and friend.... She used to live with Goran but now she lives on her own."

He was memorizing the order of hand postures so that it felt natural going along with the visualizations. "I hope and pray that it is not being sacrilegious. I devote all rituals to the service and love of God and his son Jesus. Please guide me and keep my feet upon your path."

He still was not immune to BLIPs, those brief limited intermittent psychoses. One afternoon I heard a crash. He had swept off two shelves of books in his room. At his own suggestion he dosed himself with risperidone.

He read Nietzsche.

> He writes that the closer we come to our true selves
> the more an aura of uniqueness/strangeness surrounds
> us … To truly understand something we need to be
> outside it.
>
> I think, though, that the opposite is true as well.
> Especially with esoteric knowledge to truly under-
> stand it one must be on the inside.
>
> I do think that we are often blinded by familiarity;
> when we are used to something often we do not appre-
> ciate how special/universal it is. Sometimes it takes an
> outsider to see that.

He performed his rituals, making sure he followed the complicated steps and postures while Lancaster washed himself sitting
on a chair. "I do not want the responsibility of initiating him. I do
not want a familiar." As he was writing this his left toe felt cold. He
didn't know if that was significant.

He had mixed feelings about how to proceed magickally. The
next day Lancaster vanished. Malcolm wondered if they'd done
something wrong and if it was karma but he didn't want to jump
to conclusions. First Rastus's death and now Lancaster's disappear-
ance. It was very cold. It felt weird doing meditation because he
was so sad.

He decided to cease the ceremonial magick and take it up again
in a week.

> I think I started to feel this way when I started the
> ritual of the hexagram. Some of the images include a
> cross (Osiris slain position) and I worry about it being
> blasphemous and undermining the significance of the

cross ... I want to make it clear that I serve the one true God and images are reflections of and point to that one truth.

Nothing was ever easy. To Tara he had confided that summer:

I have a great life, a supportive family, a loving girl-friend yet these beliefs that I am a bad person and the guilt accompanying them plague me. I am finding I am spending an equal time sick as healthy, if not more time sick. I am constantly fighting to believe that I am a good person yet I am weighed down. I have searched my memories of the past to see if there is anything that would warrant such extreme a feeling but there is nothing. I worry about this in that I might create false memories (I've heard this can occur in hypnosis).

My mind is often pulled into disturbing imagery but I resist this. I do not have urges to act on my be-liefs like I did when I first got sick.

I try to have hope that this illness will be cured or at least managed. It is getting to the point where I need more thorough help because I am sick of battling with myself and struggling. It has been getting worse since I saw you last Friday.

In late September he had a breakdown while working at William Ashley. No plates were broken, though. He was hitting himself, but it was only a mild version of his first bout of self-inflicting. He got home. He and I went to the Clarke, joined by Marie. Not much was done there. He was released.

Despite this relapse, and despite the downcast mental state he described to Tara, at home he seemed more alert, responsive, forward looking, hopeful, making plans to go regularly to a swimming pool. At times he seemed almost happy.

*

THAT CHRISTMAS EVE the three of us slogged through the Helena Avenue snow to Hillcrest Christian Church at the corner of Bathurst. Like his former girlfriend Marie, many of the parishioners were Filipinos, but Protestant, not Catholic. A time to bellow "O Come, All Ye Faithful" and "Joy to the World" cheerled by a tall, lanky, jovial chorister. Poinsettias adorned the sanctuary, placed "in memory of loved ones."

In hours it would be Christmas Day. Christmas, the time of eagerly anticipated childhood gifts. Not anticipation of the gifts themselves, but the festive atmosphere of giddy gladness we were all supposed — no, *compelled* — to feel. Yet Christmas had often gone wrong for me, even without the fussing and domestic flurry connected with the care of my crippled older brother. That brother, Hughie, had died long ago. Christmas no longer was a purgatory, something to be endured. Surely this one would be different from the bad, the disillusioning, Christmases of my past.

Malcolm lay on the couch on the night of a much better than average Christmas Day, his eyes fixed on *It's a Wonderful Life.*

AFTERWORD

John Pepall

THE SUMMER AFTER Malcolm died Fraser and Alison travelled to Nova Scotia to bury Malcolm's ashes next to his grandparents in the cemetery of the Bethel Presbyterian Church. Bill, and cousins, and childhood friends of Fraser joined them.

That Christmas Fraser and Alison went to New Orleans, Fraser's "favourite American city," to enjoy the food, the music, and the people.

They carried on working and living and seeing friends, including Malcolm's friends. Alison complained that people were embarrassed to talk about Malcolm while she was keen to. The annual, crowded, polyglot parties at 39 Helena in Toronto continued.

At the end of 2011 Fraser, who had worked as a lexicographer on several dictionaries, noticed a job posting by the Guangdong University of Foreign Studies seeking an English-language lexicographer to work on a dictionary of English. He summoned eminent references, applied, and was accepted.

Setting out in June 2012, he spent most of the next three years in Guangzhou, coming back for a couple of months in the winters or summers. Alison joined him for several months. He wrote regular "Letters from Guangzhou." Alison wrote some herself. He had hoped to make a book of the letters, but got no takers.

In China Fraser made new friends, many young, some of whom he would welcome to Toronto. He became a contributing editor of a bilingual journal, *Chinese Literature and Culture*, and helped young writers with editing their work in English.

Settled back in Toronto in 2016 he began writing this book.

There were new cats and a new rescue poodle.

Alison's health declined. She began to use a walker. She tried to kill herself with pills three times and in April 2018 succeeded.

Many of those who attended Malcolm's funeral eight years before returned for Alison's funeral at the same church. Back at their home Alison's wake would be the last big party there.

In August 2018 Fraser had a stroke. He made a full recovery but in October he was again in hospital for a bowel operation, and for recovery and rehabilitation remained in hospital for five weeks.

Now alone, though with boarders in what had been Malcolm's room most of the time, Fraser was out seeing friends regularly and cooked dinners for small groups of friends. He continued to write and to edit friends' work. He continued to read upward of a hundred books a year.

He continued his irregular, ecumenical church going.

In October 2019, *Bad Habits*, his last book of poetry, was launched.

In February 2020 he had another stroke but was only briefly hospitalized. When I saw him a week later he didn't even mention it.

The Covid-19 lockdown was a severe trial for Fraser. He obeyed the rules, more or less, and had himself tested, out of curiosity and to reassure friends. Though a comfortable user of his computer and the web, he hated Zoom and after a few tries gave up on it. He made the most of the easing of restrictions in the summer and fall. At Christmas he offered drop-in fare but only a couple of friends came.

When I caught up with him in hospital in January I hadn't seen him in two months. He was in good spirits and had recovered from what he described as a slight stroke. He was to have a triple bypass. We looked forward to a new lease on life. He asked me to go to his house and directed me how to get into his computer, check his email, and print out a couple of things. I was able to report that this book had been accepted for publication.

The surgeon phoned me on January 28th to report that the operation had gone well. He never recovered his wits and was most of the time in intensive care, often on a ventilator. He died two months later.

Fraser thought continually, but, except perhaps about poetry and words, he had no theories.

He makes no case in this book. After Malcolm died some asked him if he would sue Malcolm's doctors. He brushed off the idea.

His editor wanted him to write an afterword mentioning Alison's suicide, and to speculate as to whether it had been caused or hastened by Malcolm's death. Fraser was reluctant to do so. The editor also wanted him to come up with some moral of the story he tells, or to explain why he offers none. His illness and death prevented him from doing that. I cannot presume to write for him.

Fraser deeply felt the blows and sorrows he suffered, but he was indomitable. He would remain engaged, come what might. The evening before he checked himself into hospital I phoned him as

I usually did, and in reaction to a bit of gossip I retailed he let out a guffaw that I subsequently worried might have brought on his stroke.

This is *The Book of Malcolm*. It is Malcolm's life as Fraser and Alison, Malcolm's wider family, and his many friends experienced it, and as Malcolm recorded it. Fraser did not fear death, but he loved life and as a writer presented it. The moral is in the life.

*

John Pepall met Fraser at the Idler Pub in Toronto in the 1980s. They both contributed to The Idler *magazine. He was his friend, and his attorney for personal care, and he is now his executor.*